THE MUSLIM WOMAN'S HANDBOOK

By

HUDA KHATTAB

TA-HA Publishers
LONDON

Second revised edition, 1994

Reprinted: 1996, 1997, 1999, 2001, 2002, 2004, 2005

Reprinted October 2006

Published by:
Ta-Ha Publishers Ltd.
1, Wynne Road
London SW9 0BB
website: http://www.taha.co.uk/
email: sales@taha.co.uk

British Library Cataloguing in Publication Data

Khattab, Huda
Muslim Women's Handbook
1. Title
297.082

ISBN 1 897940 00 9

Typeset by JL & GA Wheatley Design, Aldershot

Printed and Bound by De-Luxe Printers Ltd,
London NW10 7NR.

بسم الله الرحمن الرحيم

Acknowledgements

My thanks must go first of all to my husband and my mother, who provided encouragement and moral and practical help during the writing of this book.

I must also thank Dr S.M. Darsh for his endless patience and sharing his wealth of knowledge with me, providing answers to many tricky questions.

Finally, I wish to thank all those sisters who have taught me since I embraced Islam; some are close and dear friends, others I may never meet again, but I pray Allah will reward them all for sharing their knowledge with me.

The first edition of this book was received with much interest, and many people contacted us to let us know of their reactions to the book. Many thanks to all those who offered constructive criticism, pointed out our errors and ambiguities, and sent words of encouragement.

May Allah guide us and keep us on the Straight Path of Islam.

Introduction

This is not just another "Women in Islam" book. You will not find lengthy discussions about why Islam is better for women, and has given them more rights, than any other faith-tradition or ism. That ground has already been covered, in great detail, by many other writers.

It may be argued that it is the menfolk who need to know the rights which Islam has given to women, and that it is high time the men gave the women the rights which Allah SWT granted fourteen hundred years ago in the Qur'an. That is a valid argument, but we cannot lay all the blame on our brothers' shoulders. It is often rightly said (admittedly usually by frustrated feminist activists!) that women can be their own worst enemy.

We should not simply demand our rights. We need to know our duties too, and do our best to fulfil them. On the Day of Judgement we will not be able to hide behind our fathers and husbands. Allah SWT will ask *us* what *we* did. Seeking knowledge is a duty for every Muslim – being female does not excuse us!

There are matters in Islam which apply specifically to women. Fathers and husbands may not be fully aware of them; our menfolk may even be embarrassed to discuss these matters, such as menstruation. It is up to us women to find out, and to teach one another. This book is an attempt to fill some of the gaps in our knowledge about these everyday matters which a Muslim woman needs to know. It grew out of a need to know more about the rules concerning menstruation, post-natal flow and non-menstrual bleeding (see Chapter Two). Hopefully it will serve as a handy reference book, although readers are advised, when in doubt, to consult with a reputable scholar.

The book does not stick to any particular "culture", as the Qur'an and Sunnah are the standard for Muslims – most cultural practices should fit within that framework (if they do not, perhaps we should think again about the way we are living). This book is aimed at born-Muslims and converts alike, of whatever ethnic or linguistic background.

I pray this book will be acceptable to Allah SWT, and of benefit to my sisters in Islam. I ask for forgiveness from Allah for any mistakes contained in it, and all I ask from my sisters is this: remember me in your prayers.

Contents

CHAPTER ONE

'Ibādah (Worship)

Introduction

In Islam, religious duties are to be performed by men and women alike. All Muslims, whether male or female, are required to pray five times daily, to fast in Ramaḍān, to pay Zakāt once a year, and to perform Hajj once in a lifetime. Having said that, however, there are some differences in the ways in which men and women are to go about performing these acts of worship, which sisters need to be aware of.

Ṣalāt (Prayer)

Women have to perform the five daily prayers, except when they are menstruating or during the period of *Nifās* (post-childbirth bleeding). Many women say that they find it too difficult to pray with babies and small children around, but we should persevere – infant antics are not an acceptable excuse for neglecting prayers, and it is only by seeing their parents pray regularly that children will learn the habit of prayer.

It has to be said that the best way to learn prayer is from another Muslim, but it is possible to learn from books or videos. In this case, it is still advisable to check with a knowledgable Muslim to be sure that the prayer has been learned correctly[1].

Prayer in the Mosque

The Islamic recommendation to offer prayers in congregation in the mosque applies to men only. The Prophet (SAAS) advised women to offer their prayers at home, in the most secluded corner of the house:

"Umm Ḥumayd Sa'idiyyah (RA) said: 'O Prophet of Allah, I desire to offer prayers under your leadership'. The Holy Prophet (SAAS) said: 'I know that, but your offering the prayer in a corner [of your house] is better than your offering it in a closed room, and your offering it in a closed room is better than your offering it in the courtyard of your house; and your offering it in the courtyard is better than your offering it in the neighbouring mosque, and your offering it in the neighbouring mosque is better than your offering it in the biggest mosque of the town'" (Imām Aḥmad and al-Ṭabarānī; similar Hadith in Abū Da'ud).

The Pakistani scholar Mawdudi has suggested that this recommendation of the Prophet (SAAS) is linked to menstruation - women who regularly attend the mosque may be conspicuous by their absence at that time of the month, and this may be a source of embarrassment. Privacy in prayer is better so that no-one need know what is what in that particular aspect of a woman's life[2]. The Prophet (SAAS) did not prevent women from attending the mosque, but he did make it clear that prayer at home is better[3].

However, women are not banned from the mosque altogether (despite certain cultural practices among Muslims!). If the intention is to pray and learn, then we can go. The Prophet (SAAS) told the men not to forbid the women if they wanted to go to the mosque:

"Do not prohibit the female slaves of Allah from coming to the mosques of Allah. When a wife of one of you asks for permission to go to the mosque, she should not be refused this permission"
(Bukhārī, Muslim).

"Do not prevent your women from coming to the mosques, though their houses are better for them"
(Abu Da'ud)

If we want to claim our right to go to the mosque, we have to observe certain rules of behaviour, in particular, there is to be no mixing with men. In mosques with a "ladies' gallery", this is easy to do. Other mosques may screen off an area for women to pray in. It's interesting to note that at the time of the Prophet (SAAS), the mosque was a simple, single-storey building; the men occupied the front rows, and the women were at the back[4].

The clothes we wear in the mosque must also be correct: all the body and hair – except the hands and face – must be covered properly, and no make-up or perfume should be worn. We shouldn't make the mistake of thinking that if our dress is "Traditional Muslim Dress" it will be acceptable; shalwar-khameez, saris, long skirts and the like are not acceptable if they are tight or low-cut or reveal parts of the body such as arms, stomach or legs, etc. The intention in coming to the mosque should be to worship and to learn, not to show off or draw attention to ourselves.

It is interesting to note that women were banned from coming to the mosque by the Khalif 'Umar (RA) and even by 'A'ishah herself (RA). 'Umar (RA) imposed this ban because society had deteriorated to such an extent that it was not befitting for women to go out to the mosque, especially at night. The women of Madinah, resenting this ban, approached 'A'ishah (RA), but she backed 'Umar up, telling them: "If the Prophet (SAAS) knew what 'Umar knows, he would not have granted you permission to go out (to the mosque)"[5].

Obviously, Muslims today are faced with a society much worse than that of 'Umar and 'A'ishah (RA)! Hence the ban on women in mosques among some Muslim communities. However, as the Nigerian scholar Abdur Rahman Doi points out, the Prophet (SAAS) *did* grant women permission to attend the mosque, and he suggests that this practice should be revived – subject to the proper conditions of dress, etc, so that women can learn more about Islam, encourage one another, etc.[6]

Congregational prayer at home

The rule about men praying in the front rows and women praying at the back applies to prayer at home, too. Even a husband and wife shouldn't form one row in prayer.

Praying *en famille* is a particularly good way of reinforcing family ties and of setting a good example to younger children: most children, including toddlers, will want to join in, and will learn the movements of the prayer without too much difficulty.

Leading the Prayer

A woman cannot lead a mixed congregation in prayer, but where there are only women present, one of them can lead the others. Thus, although we don't have to attend prayers in the mosque, we need not miss out on the benefits and reward of congregational prayer.

When a woman leads others in prayer, she should stand in the middle of the row, not out in front like a male Imam. If there is only one other woman present, she should stand to the right of the "Imam". The woman on the right should recite the *Iqāma* (call immediately preceding prayer)[7].

Jum'ah (Friday) Prayer

Attending Jum'ah prayer is obligatory on men, but not on women. This makes allowances for our other obligations: for example, it's difficult to attend the mosque with babies and small children in tow. There is also the question of menstruation and possible embarrassment when otherwise regular attendance is interrupted (see above). However, we are not forbidden to attend the mosque (see above also), so the decision whether or not to attend Jum'ah prayers is very much an individual one, depending on circumstances, other commitments, facilities available in the mosque, etc.

One important thing to remember when attending Friday prayers is that the *Khuṭbah* (sermon) is as much a part of the observance as the prayer itself; it is forbidden to talk during the Khuṭbah, and take the opportunity to learn from it instead[8].

Eid Prayers

Although the Eid Prayers are Sunnah (not obligatory) for both men and women, those of us living in a non-Muslim country should make the most of the opportunity to gather together and celebrate with large numbers of our fellow-Muslims. The Prophet (SAAS) positively encouraged all women to attend and share the joy of Eid. This extends even to menstruating women, although they cannot join in the prayer, of course – but they can still join in the *Takbīrāt*.

> Umm Atiyyah (RA) narrated: "The Messenger of Allah (SAAS) ordered us to bring old women, young girls and middle aged women on both the Eids to the Eid prayer place, but those women who are having their monthly period should not join the Eid prayer"
> (Bukhari, Muslim)

> Umm Atiyyah (RA) narrated: "On the occasion of every Eid an order came from the Messenger of Allah SAW that we should also bring the menstruating women to the Eid prayer place, so that they could join in with the other women to say the Takbirs"
> (Bukhari)

Of course, when we attend the Eid prayers, the same rules of decorum in the mosque apply: we should be dressed in correct Ḥijāb, and should avoid mixing with the men.

Ṣawm (Fasting)

Fasting during the month of Ramaḍān is compulsory on all Muslims:

> "O you who believe! Fasting is prescribed to you as it was prescribed to those before you, that you may (learn) self restraint"
> (al-Baqarah 2:183).

Grammatically speaking, the masculine plural used here in Arabic refers to females as well as to males.

The Islamic fast means a total abstinence from all food, drink, tobacco (for smokers) and conjugal relations (for those who are married), between the hours of sunrise and sunset.

Women are not allowed to fast during menstruation and post-natal bleeding. Any fasts missed must be made up at a later date.

During illness, pregnancy and breast-feeding, a woman may be excused from fasting, but it is better to fast if you are able to and there is no medical risk. Again, any fasts you miss have to be made up later on.

There are many "optional" fasts in Islam too, which all Muslims, male and female, are encouraged to observe, following the Sunnah of the Prophet

(SAAS). However, a married woman should not observe an "optional" fast without the permission of her husband. This is because she should not refuse his advances, which she would have to do if she were fasting (for more details see the section on obligations and the sexual relationship in the chapter on Marriage, p42–43).

Zakāt

In Islam, a woman's wealth is her own, and she is responsible to no-one except Allah for how she disposes of it. If the amount of wealth makes you liable to pay Zakāt, you must make sure it is paid.

Zakāt is payable on gold and silver jewellery, and on cash (including money in bank accounts, and money earned in rent for buildings one owns). The rate is 2.5%, and Zakāt should be paid once a year[9].

Ḥajj

A woman is required to perform Ḥajj just as a man is, but she must be accompanied by her husband or a Maḥrem (father, brother, son, etc.). Women who are without such an escort are not in fact under obligation to perform Ḥajj, but according to some schools of thought (Māliki, Shāfi'ī) may go to Ḥajj with a large group, such as those organized by Muslim travel agents – in this case the group itself constitutes the Maḥrem[10].

As Ḥajj is not a day-to-day matter, it will not be dealt with in detail in this book. Guides to Ḥajj are available in Islamic bookshops, and any reputable company organizing trips to Makkah should also be able to advise.

Reading Qur'an

Recitation and memorization of the Qur'an is considered an act of worship in Islam, as much for women as for men – although women should not recite aloud in mixed gatherings. Of course, women can read aloud in female-only gatherings, and such meetings are to be encouraged; if there is no group in your area, why not start one? You don't need a vast crowd of people – two or three can learn together.

For information on touching or reciting Qur'an during menstruation, see the chapter on *Ṭahārah* (page 10).

Jihād

Jihād is often described as the sixth pillar of Islam. The common translation "Holy War" is quite inaccurate; the true meaning is struggle and striving in the path of Allah SWT. This need not necessarily take the form of armed combat on the battlefield! Daily life involves Jihād as well, for example the expression *Jihād al-Nafs* (the Jihād against the self) refers to the constant internal battle to control and overcome one's baser nature and bad habits such as laziness, bad temper and the like.

At the time of the Prophet (SAAS), some women accompanied the men when they went out to fight, but their role was primarily one of support, not combat. They had to seek permission from the Prophet (SAAS), and their First Aid and other work was mostly confined to the men of their own family or tribe (i.e. husbands or Maḥrem); they did not tend others unless it was absolutely necessary, and even then contact was kept to the bare minimum – the same conditions as would apply to the giving or receiving of any kind of medical treatment. When asked about Jihād for women, the Prophet (SAAS) said that their Jihād was Ḥajj, i.e. the reward of women performing Ḥajj would be equivalent to that of a man going out to fight in Jihād. Ayesha (RA) sought permission to go out and fight, and the Prophet (SAAS) told her, "The Jihād of you women is Ḥajj"; on another occasion she asked whether Jihād was compulsory for women too, and was told, "Yes, Jihād which does not include fighting is obligatory on them. It is the Ḥajj and the 'Umrah" (Ibn Mājah)[11].

Pregnancy and childbirth may also be regarded in some sense as a form of Jihād, because of the Hadith which describes the mother who dies in childbirth as being a martyr (*shahīd*): "A woman who dies in childbirth together with the baby becomes a martyr" (Aḥmad, al-Tabarānī)[12].

Summary

All acts of worship in Islam are as essential for women as for men. There are slight differences, both in the way they are to be performed (such as variations in the movements of Ṣalāt) and in emphasis (ways of Jihād for women may differ from those for men). Being female in no way lessens our responsibility or opportunity for performing acts of worship.

Notes

1. Although some Muslims observe slight differences for men and women in the prayer, it has been pointed out that the Prophet's (SAAS) command "Pray as you have seen me praying" includes men as well as women. See al-Albani, *The Prophet's Prayer Described,* p 93.
2. Mawdudi, *Purdah and the Status of Woman in Islam,* p 208.
3. Doi, *Women in Shari'ah,* p 29.
4. Mawdudi, op. cit, p 210.
5. Doi, op. cit, p 29–30.
6. Ibid.
7. Rahman, *Role of Muslim Women in Society,* p 289.
8. Abdalati, *Islam in Focus,* p 87.
9. The rules of Zakat are rather too complicated to go into here, but more details can be obtained from a booklet entitled *Zakah – The Religious Tax of Islam (Brief Guidelines),* by Abdul Rehman Ansari, (IPCI), 481 Coventry Road, Birmingham B10 0JS.
10. Dr. S.M. Darsh, unpublished answer to a query from a reader of *Usra – The Muslim Family Magazine.*
11. Rahman, *Role of Muslim Women,* p 184.
12. See Schleifer, *Motherhood in Islam,* p 2 ff for fuller discussion of the Islamic concept of pregnancy and childbirth as Jihad.

CHAPTER TWO

Ṭahārah (Purity and Cleanliness)

In Arabic, the word *Ṭahārah* carries the meaning of purity, in both a physical and spiritual sense. In this chapter we are concerned with the physical aspects of the term, in particular regarding menstruation and post-natal bleeding.

Before *Ṣalāt,* a person must perform ablution, either *Wuḍū'* or *Ghusl* depending on the nature of the *Najāsah* (impurity). In brief, passing wind, urine or stools, or vomiting, necessitates Wuḍū'; Ghusl should be performed following sexual intercourse, emission of seminal fluid, and the ceasing of menstruation and post-natal bleeding.[1]

Obviously, the areas of special concern to women are menstruation and post-natal bleeding, and it is these which will be dealt with in more detail in this chapter.

Ḥayḍ (menstruation)

Ḥayḍ is the Arabic term referring to the period or monthly flow of blood. When a girl starts having periods, she is regarded in Islam as *Mukallaf* (adult, responsible), and must perform all the regular duties of Islam, such as prayer, fasting, etc. There is no set age of becoming Mukallaf as it varies from one individual to the next, and is determined by hereditary factors, diet, climate, etc.

The menstrual flow is described by scholars as having certain characteristics: the blood is red, thick and has a distinct, unpleasant odour. Other types of discharge may be regarded as *Istiḥāḍah* (see below).

Menstruation is not regarded in Islam as a "curse"[2], but as one of several normal bodily functions which render a person in need of ablution before he/she can pray (see above). Menstruation is one of these functions: there are things you cannot do at this time, and at the end of the period you must perform Ghusl before resuming normal activity. It does not mean that the woman is considered dirty; rather the Qur'an describes menstruation as a ''hurt" (see al-Baqarah 2:222), so the restrictions on normal activity at this time are to be regarded as a mercy and a relief.

During your period, you cannot:

(a) Pray, i.e. perform Ṣalāt; *Du'ā* is acceptable at all times. The Ṣalāt missed does not have to be made up later on.
(b) Fast, but any obligatory fasts missed must be made up later on.
(c) Perform *Ṭawāf* (circumambulation of the Ka'bah during Hajj or 'Umrah).
(d) Have sexual intercourse; embracing, kissing, etc are acceptable – it is the act of coition itself which is forbidden.
(e) Touch a *Muṣ-ḥaf* except for purposes of learning or teaching it to others. Some scholars (e.g. Shāfi'īs), say there is no restriction on touching books which contain Qur'ānic texts in Arabic, where these form less than 50% of the text – an example would be a translation and commentary on the Qur'ān, such as that by Yūsuf 'Alī[3]. There is no restriction on reciting small portions of the Qur'ān without touching it, during one's period[4].

Minimum and maximum length of period

Some women suffer from irregular and/or long periods, which may lead to confusion as to whether or not one should pray. The scholars regard the normal period as being six or seven days; the minimum is one day and one night; the maximum is ten or fifteen days. Any bleeding in excess of this is regarded as Istiḥāḍah (see below).

A woman may perform Ghusl at the end of her period, then find a "spot" of some discharge; if it is yellowish or brownish in colour, it is of no consequence. The menstrual blood (Ḥayḍ) is red in colour, as described above. There is no particular virtue in trying to hasten the end of the period; some women naturally have a longer period, so you can't be blamed if, for example, your period lasts ten days while another sister's only lasts for seven – you are under no obligation to pray etc while your period is on, in fact you could be doing wrong by seeking to pray before you're actually supposed to! The early Muslim women came across the same problems, as can be seen in the following Aḥādīth:

> Some women used to send the pads of cotton with traces of yellowish discharge to Ayeshah RA (for her verdict as to whether their menstruation had ended or not). And Ayeshah would say: "Do not hurry until you see the cotton pad is white (i.e. that menstruation has completely ceased)". The daughter of Zayd ibn Thābit was told that some women used to ask for candles at midnight to see whether menstruation has stopped or not. At that, the daughter of Zayd said that the ladies (the wives of the Prophet's companions) had never done so, and she blamed them (the women who were doing this)
> (Bukhari)

> Umm 'Atiyyah (RA) narrated: "We never considered yellowish discharge as a thing of importance (i.e. as menstrual flow)"
> (Bukhari)

Istiḥāḍah (Non-menstrual flow)

Scholars distinguish between menstrual bleeding (Ḥayḍ), when a woman may not pray, fast etc., and non-menstrual bleeding Istiḥāḍah), when a woman must continue with her regular Islamic duties. This non-menstrual flow may follow on from a period, or occur at other times of the month. A woman in this condition should wash and perform Wuḍū' before each prayer. Other kinds of discharge, such as the clear mucus which is always present in the vagina and which may increase at the time of ovulation, and the yellowish or greenish discharge which may indicate an infection (such as thrush), are also not considered to be Ḥayḍ.

The following is a guide to help distinguish Istiḥāḍah from Ḥayḍ:

(1) If your cycle is usually regular, take that as your standard. For example, if your period usually lasts for seven days, regard the eighth and subsequent days as Istiḥāḍah, and resume prayers, etc.

(2) If you can detect a difference between menstrual and non-menstrual blood, perform Ghusl and resume your Islamic duties after the menstrual flow ceases, even if there is still some kind of blood.

(3) Go by the pattern of your immediate female relatives (mother or sister).

If you know the usual number of days of their period, regard that as Ḥayḍ and any excess as Istiḥāḍah.

(4) You can follow the maximum number of days laid down by scholars – ten or fifteen according to different schools of thought. If your cycle is usually quite short, regard ten days as the maximum; count fifteen days if your usual cycle is longer. If bleeding continues after that time, regard it as Istiḥāḍah, perform Ghusl and resume normal duties.

It has been known for women to have a very short gap between bleeds: this is confusing, and may even be distressing. The shortest gap between menstrual periods is 15 days according to most scholars (13 according to the Ḥanbali *Madhhab*). There is no upper time limit, as it is well known that women may go for months without a period, especially if they are severely over- or under-weight[5].

According to Islam there is no Ḥayḍ in pregnancy. It has been known for women to bleed every month, like a light period, during pregnancy. In this rare event, the woman should pray and fast etc., as normal: this bleeding is regarded as Istiḥāḍah[6].

IMPORTANT: Apart from the discomfort and inconvenience caused, irregular, heavy or lengthy bleeding may be indicative of an underlying health problem. If you find yourself in this situation, it is strongly recommended that you consult your doctor as soon as possible.

Nifās (Post-natal bleeding)

This is the bleeding which follows childbirth and may go on for as long as several weeks. There is no minimum period of *Nifās*; if you happen to stop bleeding straightaway, you should perform Ghusl and resume your normal duties. It is more normal for the discharge to continue for several days or weeks; the scholars define the maximum period of Nifās as forty days. Interestingly enough, this forty-day period is not so far removed from the six-week post-partum period regarded as the norm in western medicine.

The Nifās changes from a heavy, red bleeding in the beginning to a lighter discharge towards the end. As long as discharge is still flowing, it is regarded as Nifās, whatever the colour. If the discharge ceases for 24 hours, you may assume that Nifās has ended, and perform Ghusl. But if the discharge resumes within up to 4 days (as long as you are still within the 40-day maximum period), it is still regarded as Nifās, so you should stop praying etc, until the discharge stops again[7].

When the discharge stops, or at the end of the forty-day period (whichever comes first), you should perform Ghusl and resume your normal duties of prayer, fasting, etc.

Personal hygiene

There are also matters of everyday personal hygiene which a Muslim woman needs to be aware of. These are:

(1) Cleaning of the private parts after using the toilet. Using tissue paper is not enough – this area must be washed with water after passing water or faeces. (Of course, tissue paper may be used as well)[8].

(2) Removal of body hair: pubic and underarm hair must be removed regularly. Plucking of underarm hair is recommended, but it may be shaved; shaving is recommended for pubic hair[9]. Removing hair from the legs is acceptable, as is removing excess hair from the face – but plucking the eyebrows to shape and thin them is not allowed[10].

(3) Trimming the nails: nails should be kept short and neat; the western fashion of long fingernails is not acceptable for a Muslim woman[11].

Summary

Women experience monthly periods and bleeding after childbirth, both of which affect our performance of normal Islamic duties; other types of bleeding and discharge may occur, which do not prevent us from praying, etc. We need to know the difference, so that we do not make the mistake of trying to perform duties when it is forbidden to do so, or of neglecting them when in fact we should be carrying on as normal.

Notes

1. See Badawi, *Ṭahārah*, p 9 ff (Wudu), p 18 ff (Ghusl), for a more detailed discussion.

2. Some western women refer colloquially to menstruation as "the curse" – a reflection of the popular notion that menstruation is the "curse" inflicted on Eve and her daughters as punishment for tempting Adam to disobey God. Of course Islam totally rejects this idea!
3. Badawi, *Ṭahārah,* p 16, footnote 33.
4. Ibid.
5. al-Sabbāgh, p 11.
6. Ibid.
7. Darsh, response to author's query.
8. Khan, *Personal Hygiene in Islam,* p 10, Ta-Ha Publishers.
9. al-Kaysi, *Morals and Manners in Islam,* p 67.
10. Darsh, "Questions of Faith", *Usra – The Muslim Family Magazine,* Jumādā al-Ū lā 1412 AH/ November-December 1991.
11. al-Kaysi, op.cit., p 67.

CHAPTER THREE

Ḥijāb

Ḥijāb is just one very important aspect of a Muslim woman's life. The word, as generally understood nowadays, refers to the woman's Islamic dress; it often refers specifically to the head-cover or scarf.

The fact that there is more to Ḥijāb than clothes is often overlooked. Adherence to the Islamic dress code should be accompanied by correct Islamic behaviour. We can speak in terms of "external" Ḥijāb (clothes) and "internal" Ḥijāb (attitude and behaviour)[1].

The External Ḥijāb

There are certain conditions which we must follow if our dress is to be considered Islamic. No particular style has been dictated – you can wear whatever you like as long as it falls within the definition of Islamic dress: climate, tradition, personal taste and, yes, fashion, may all play a part. [There are fashions in shalwar khameez and other styles of Muslim dress, as much as in the world of western clothes. Fashion isn't a problem as long as we don't follow blindly; we should have the sense to realize when fashions are not Islamically acceptable, and "dare" to be unfashionable at those times].

The conditions which make clothing Islamic are as follows[2]:

(1) It should cover the whole head and body, except the face and hands: this means that the neck, forearms, ears and any earrings worn must be covered too. Some schools of thought say that the feet may be left bare, but all agree that the legs must be covered.

(2) The clothing should not be in itself an adornment: it should not attract

men's attention to the woman's beauty. This is widely taken to mean that dazzling bright colours, glittery decorations and material interwoven with shiny thread should be avoided. [Such items may, of course, be worn in the home – these criteria apply to what is worn outside the home and/or in the presence of non-Mahrem men].

(3) It should be thick enough to conceal the colour of the skin: translucent and "see-thru" fabrics are not suitable.

(4) It should be loose enough to conceal the shape of the body: clingy, "body-hugging" styles which delineate the contours of the body are not acceptable.

(5) The clothes should not be perfumed.

(6) The clothes should not resemble men's clothing. [Items of clothing, such as trousers, which are worn by both men and women, should be of a woman's style].

(7) The clothing should not make you stand out – it should not be of such bright colours or way-out design as to attract attention. For this reason, some Muslims advise that Muslim women in the UK should avoid the more ''exotic" forms of Muslim dress – such as Arabian abayas or Iranian chadors (kinds of cloaks) – in favour of adapted versions of western dress, such as a skirt suit comprising a loose fitting, long-line jacket and long skirt of a smart cut. This is very much a matter of individual conscience, but this writer would advise taking the climate and one's field of work (whether inside or outside the home) into account when deciding on the type of Ḥijāb to wear: what suits a stay-at-home mother with plenty of help in the house in Arabia may not be appropriate for a harrassed working mother in rainy Manchester!

(8) It should not be similar to the costume of non-Muslims. One of the functions of Ḥijāb is to identify the wearer as a Muslim who is proud (in the best sense) of her Islam. In particular, we should avoid wearing clothes which imitate the religious dress of others – the fashion among some "Asian" Muslim women of wearing Hindu-style dots on the forehead is an example of such unacceptable trends.

(9) It should not be a "dress of fame or vanity"; this means that it should not be ostentatious, encrusted with gems, woven with gold and silver threads and the like.

The women at the time of the Prophet (SAAS) used to have outer garments – the *jilbaab* (cloak) and *khimār* (head-cover)[3] – which they would don whenever they went out. Historically, different forms of outer garment have evolved throughout the Muslim world, such as the *'abaya* in Arabia, *chador* in Iran, *burqa* in Pakistan, etc. These may not be suited to the British climate, but it is possible to cover with an outer-garment here – longer length macs and coats of appropriate styles and colours may be used, and in many parts of the country it is possible to buy, or have sewn, the kind of garment known in modern parlance as a "jilbab", i.e. a loose, coat-like garment, which nowadays is well-known among muslims of all backgrounds.

It must be noted here that the Dupatta, the filmy headcover often sold with a shalwar-khameez, is not acceptable as Ḥijāb; draping a virtually transparent dupatta over the top of the head, leaving long hair showing underneath it, does not do the job! The dupatta should be folded once or twice, until it becomes opaque, and then worn in such a way as to cover all the hair; if this isn't possible, it's better to use another scarf altogether. If you're very fashion-conscious, you may be reassured by the fact that Arabian-style scarves are very popular nowadays – this writer has frequently seen them worn with shalwar-khameez – and are quite widely available in the UK.

There is a certain amount of debate among scholars as to the extent of the covering. Some (mostly Shafi'i and Hanbali) favour covering the face and hands, too. The Maliki Madhhab considers the whole body – except the face and hands – to be *'Awrah* [that which must be covered]. The Hanafis suggest likewise; later Hanafi scholars have allowed uncovering the feet too, but other scholars have suggested that this is an unfounded ruling[4].

From this we can understand that covering all the body – except the hands and face is the *absolute minimum* extent of Ḥijāb. It is quite clear that all of the hair, the neck and arms must be covered.

Some people – Muslims as well as non-Muslims – may feel that wearing Ḥijāb prevents women from doing a proper job: this is not so. One is reminded of the objections raised when schoolgirls in Manchester wanted to wear Ḥijāb: one claim was that the scarves would pose a fire risk in the chemistry lab. This isn't so – the scarves can easily be tucked into the neck of a blouse or jumper: end of problem!

Others wonder if you can really be a lawyer/doctor/manager/journalist/ whatever in "long flowing robes"! Admittedly, a "floral tent" of a dress would look out of place in the City, but you can look businesslike and professional in Ḥijāb. If you're handy with a needle, you can adopt most patterns, or find a dressmaker who will adapt and lengthen a pattern. Failing that, if you look hard enough in the shops you will find suitable clothes – sometimes you can buy a dress several sizes too big, which will then come loose and long enough to qualify as Ḥijāb; if you're short and fashions are long, you'll end up with full-length skirts – taller women can always try specialist shops for the same result, as an average-height woman buying clothes designed for tall women will also find herself with long dresses and skirts! Shops catering for a particular look (such as Laura Ashley) may also offer long clothes. (Hint: some of these "specialist" shops may be rather expensive, so watch out for sales!). With a little effort, you can look businesslike enough to take on the world – without sacrificing your Islamic principles.

Wearing Ḥijāb isn't really such a problem – the practicalities of obtaining suitable clothes have been tackled above. Society at large is getting more and more used to seeing Muslim women in Ḥijāb, in the street, in shops and offices, on TV and in the media. It's not as "strange" as it was, say, ten years ago. The first few days and weeks of wearing Ḥijāb are admittedly the hardest, but the longer you persevere, the easier it gets, until wearing it is second nature, and you begin to wonder how you could ever go out without it.

The Internal Ḥijāb

The idea of "Ḥijāb" doesn't only apply to clothes. There is a whole attitude and way of behaving which goes with the dress code, and which is the ideal behaviour of the Muslim woman. This is the attitude of *Haya'* (modesty, shyness, bashfulness) which the Prophet (SAAS) described as being a part of faith[5]. Whether a Muslim woman wears Ḥijāb or not, she should still strive to adopt this Islamic behaviour; the dress-code is just one part of being a Muslim woman. This attitude is often at odds with the normally acceptable behaviour in the West (or perhaps that should be the other way round!) so for many of us who have grown up here, whether born-Muslim or reverts, it will take a conscious effort to stick to it.

The Voice

The voice is regarded by some scholars as being *'Awrah,* as it may be attractive to men; other scholars disagree, after all the Hadith literature cites many instances when the wives of the Prophet (SAAS) spoke to non-Maḥrem men, for example when conveying religious teaching and the like (they were major sources of Aḥādīth because, naturally, they knew a great deal of the Prophet's life). Certainly, talking in a soft, alluring voice or, conversely, talking and laughing too loudly can put across the wrong message. The Qur'an forbids using a soft voice:

> "... If you do fear (Allah), be not too complaisant of speech, lest one in whose heart is a disease should be moved with desire: but speak a speech (that is) just" (al-Aḥzāb 33:32)

This Āyah was addressed primarily to the wives of the Prophet (SAAS) but the wisdom contained in it is valuable for all women. In some Muslim cultures, raising one's voice or laughing out loud in the hearing of men, even if they are in another room, is severely disapproved of: it is better to err on the side of caution in this matter.

The best advice for Muslim women in this country, where we often have to deal with non-Maḥrem men (teachers, doctors, shop-keepers, etc.) is to control one's voice and speech. The tone should be polite and businesslike, not soft, alluring, flirtatious or giggly. The talk should be restricted to the business in hand – there is no need to indulge in idle chit-chat: such conversations may easily wander onto unsuitable topics, especially in this society where everything is discussed frankly and openly (often too openly, as far as Islamic standards go). We also need to watch our laughter. Islam does not forbid smiling, laughter and joking, but such merriment is often taken to extremes in the West: it is this excess which is condemned in Islam, which is the Deen of moderation and balance. We should not giggle and laugh out loud in the presence or hearing of non-Maḥrem men.

Mixing

Free mixing of the sexes is to be avoided as much as possible. Of course we live in a free-mixing society, where few institutions are segregated (indeed, the situation may be just as difficult even in some Muslim countries which follow western models!). It is possible for a Muslim woman to study or work and not get involved in the unacceptable aspects of college and office life. We will have to speak to male colleagues at times, but this can be kept to a minimum and restricted to "business" talk. Flirting is common in the West, but men would soon get the idea, from a Muslim woman's dress and manner that she does not wish to play the game. Indeed, sexual harassment has been described as *unwelcome* contact, so (in theory at least!) having made our position clear, we should have the right to legal protection from such hassles. Many Muslim women have found that their colleagues will respect them for their beliefs, especially if you take the trouble to explain the whys and wherefores without being aggressive or defensive. Often there may be less hassle than you feared; in those unfortunate cases where a colleague is being openly hostile and trying to cause problems, there are always procedures for dealing with such harrassment (racial, sexual or just general): union officials, welfare officers and sympathetic superiors are the people to approach for help.

Pubs and the like

Bars and pubs are another feature of British life which holds pitfalls for the unwary Muslim, male or female. Less sensitive colleagues may overdo the jokes about alcohol and abstinence – it's best to ignore this if you can, however irritating it is. Others may genuinely want to include you in the group, and may invite you to join them in the bar at lunchtime; they may even know that you don't drink alcohol and won't try to force you: "It's OK, you can have orange juice". What they – and many Muslims – don't realize is that just avoiding booze is not enough. It's Ḥarām to sit with people who are drinking; It is also Ḥarām to sell alcohol, or even to serve or pass it to another person; the Prophet (SAAS) curse those who deal with alcohol in any way[6]. There is a further consideration to be borne in mind. People tend to judge Islam by whatever they see Muslims doing: however unscientific this attitude may be, it's a fact of life, and if we are known as Muslims, especially if we wear Ḥijāb, we are ambassadors for Islam in this society. Most people know that Muslims aren't supposed to drink; they also assume that when a person goes into a pub, the purpose is to partake of alcohol. You might know you're only going to have a Coke, but other people don't: they will put two and two together and make five – "there goes another so-called Muslim: what a hypocrite! It can't be much of a religion if that's how its followers behave!"

Handshakes and touching

The British are famous for being an undemonstrative race, which is a relief for Muslims! In Islam, when it comes to non-Mahrem men, the rule is don't touch – even shaking hands is, strictly speaking, forbidden. In Britain, the handshake, one of the few occasions where touching is universally acceptable, carries a lot of weight in terms of social behaviour and etiquette. Muslim men should know better, and shouldn't offer their hand, but sometimes need to be politely reminded of what's what. In general, non-Muslim men will be unaware of the Islamic custom – a few may ask, and can be told, diplomatically. In other cases, where the intention is almost certainly nothing more than an attempt to be polite, you have to make your mind up there and then; for example, if you're in an interview and it's your prospective boss or tutor who's holding out his hand, it may well be more prudent to shake his hand as quickly as is acceptable, so as not to cause undue offence. However, it is still better to avoid shaking hands if you can do so without appearing too impolite. We should take every opportunity to get this message across, in a diplomatic way, so that further embarrassment and compromise can be avoided.

Other kinds of touching which may be common in an environment such as an office (an arm around the shoulder, playfully touching the hand or arm, etc), are totally unacceptable, and you should make this clear, as diplomatically – but as firmly – as possible. If the person concerned still doesn't get the message, you will need to take a tougher approach; such incidents have, in the past, been proven to be a form of sexual harassment, when a woman has made it clear that she finds touching offensive but the man has not respected her wishes (as mentioned above, sexual harrassment is described as unwelcome contact, which obviously is an individual matter, and you have the right to voice your feelings and wishes for respect).

A case where the usual rules regarding covering, touching, etc., are waived, is in the case of medical examinations. While it is always preferable to be seen by a female doctor, it is not always possible; a Muslim woman is allowed to be seen by a male doctor if necessary. This subject is discussed more fully in the chapter on Health (see page 51f).

"Purdah"

Finally, we need to give some consideration to the word "Purdah", which is often used in connection with the idea of "Ḥijāb" (the two words are sometimes used interchangeably). "Purdah" conjures up pictures of women enveloped in voluminous robes and confined to the four walls of the house. This is the practice in some Muslim countries, and indeed among some Muslims in Britain. In fact Islam is not so extreme; women are allowed to go out for any legitimate need, including education, work, medical treatment and the like, but a Muslim woman's life should centre on the home. Once you have finished your business outside, you should go home as quickly as possible. Hanging around in streets, markets, or places of amusement is not acceptable behaviour for a Muslim woman. Our homes are not meant to be our prisons, but our lives are certainly meant to be home-based.

Summary

"Ḥijāb isn't just a fashion, it's an attitude!" While clothes are important, we have to remember that there's more to being a Muslim woman than just wearing a scarf and a long dress. The clothes should remind us to behave in an Islamic manner at all times, wherever we are. Sisters who are not yet wearing Ḥijāb (for whatever reason – it is a big step, especially in Britain) can still work towards the "inner Ḥijāb" – very often the "outer Ḥijāb" will follow in due course.

Notes

1. I am indebted to Hutchinson, *The Ḥijāb in Classical and Modern Muslim Scholarship*, ch 2, for the idea of "outer" and "inner" Ḥijāb.
2. Badawi, *Muslim Woman's Dress according to the Qur'ān and Sunnah*, passim.
3. See Badawi, op. cit., p 6f.
4. al-Kanadi, *The Islamic Ruling Regarding Women's Dress*, p 16–17.
5. Ibid., p 20.
6. Hadith narrated by al-Tirmidhi and Ibn Majah. See Karim, *al-Hadis*, Vol. 2, p 572.

CHAPTER FOUR

Social Life

Islam is not an all-work-and-no-play way of life. The Prophet (SAAS) recognized that people need leisure and relaxation, in order to "recharge their batteries", but leisure need not – indeed should not – be spent in useless or destructive pursuits, and it should not take up a disproportionate amount of our time.

Relaxation is not at odds with piety and dignity. The Prophet (SAAS) prayed and engaged in *'Ibādah* more than anyone, but he also enjoyed good things, smiled and joked gently with people, and used to pray to Allah for protection from grief and distress (Abu Da'ud).

The Companions of the Prophet also followed this advice, and counselled others to do so too. 'Ali ibn Abi Ṭālib (RA) said: "Minds get tired, as do bodies, so treat them with humour" ... "Refresh your minds from time to time, for a tired mind becomes blind". And Abū'l-Dardā' (RA) said: "I entertain my heart with something trivial in order to make it stronger in the service of the Truth"[1].

Sport and Exercise

Islam advocates care of the body as well as of the soul! The Prophet (SAAS) advised his followers to practise certain sports so that they would be fit and ready for action at any time – archery, horse riding and swimming in particular were encouraged[2]. He raced with his wife Ayeshah (RA) on occasion[3], and also let her watch a display of spear play in the mosque with him[4].

From these episodes we can be sure that physical fitness is encouraged for all Muslims, and that watching sport is acceptable for Muslim women as long as no lewdness is involved and that no Islamic observances are broken, for example, it wouldn't be a good idea for a woman to go and watch an event on her own – it would be better to go with her husband, a Maḥrem or a group of people.

When it comes to taking part in sport, the main problem we encounter is that most sports facilities in Britain are mixed, and the kind of dress encouraged or even required (shorts, T-shirts, leotards, swimming costumes, etc) is not acceptable Islamically. However, there is hope! There is an increasing awareness that many women – not just Muslims – would prefer an all-female environment and a relaxation of the clothing rules; for example, overweight women may feel shy of mixed sport sessions and would rather not wear a leotard or swimsuit. In many areas there are already female-only sports activities; if there is nothing where you live, you could bring it to the attention of the people in charge of facilities (the local council, management of leisure centres, etc) – unless they know there is a demand, they cannot cater for it. It is permissible for Muslim women to attend sports activities with non-Muslim women, but it is probably better to stick to Ḥijā b as far as possible, if only because one doesn't know the other women very well[5]. There's no need to wear a leotard or shorts: baggy jogging trousers and a long loose top don't restrict your movements, as many Muslim women who've tried it will tell you. For swimming, western style swimsuits are out, as the thighs are considered 'Awrah even among women; leggings or Bermuda (knee-length) shorts and a T-shirt or leotard, or even a "Victorian" swimsuit, if you can buy or make one, will keep you covered while not restricting your movements too much.

Almost all sports can be recommended, as long as the facilities meet with Islamic requirements. Swimming and aerobics/keep fit seem especially popular with women, but they are not the only sports available. The aim of sports should be to develop stamina, agility, physical strength, etc.: all sports do this in varying measure, so it's worthwhile looking around for something that suits you.

Music and singing

It seems that all human societies make music of some sort, and music as such is not entirely forbidden in Islam. However, as with all other areas of human life, Islam has defined the limits within which we may involve ourselves in this area of activity.

The Imams of the four schools of thought agreed that musical instruments are prohibited[6] and that Muslims should avoid listening to such music, especially if the words and/or manner of singing are lewd or suggestive – which rules out virtually all pop music! However, there is no blame attached to hearing music such as that "piped" into supermarkets or used as signature tunes on TV and radio.

The only musical instrument approved by the Prophet (SAAS) is a kind of hand-drum called a *daff*, which resembles a tambourine without the rattles. Singing (without instrumental accompaniment, apart from the daff) was recommended on certain occasions, namely on Eid and at weddings, but women may only sing in front of a female audience. The lyrics of any song they sing should be Islamically acceptable, and there should be nothing suggestive either in the song or the way it is sung.

Innocent forms of singing, such as to relieve boredom on a journey, or to amuse or calm a small child, are permitted – within the Islamic limits as mentioned above. Songs which encourage Islamic deeds are also allowed, in moderation and on appropriate occasions.

In short, our involvement with such entertainment should be minimal – this is very different from the West where music is part and parcel of daily life and popular culture is more or less defined in terms of music! We should divert ourselves towards more acceptable alternatives such as reciting and listening to the Qur'an, Islamic songs, dhikr and healthy sports activities[7].

Singing may be allowed at certain times. At the time of the Prophet (SAAS), some women used to sing at Eid and at weddings[8]. Again, the words should be acceptable Islamically, and women shouldn't sing in front of mixed company or in the hearing of men.

Movies and cinemas

Movies are a popular form of entertainment throughout the world, and especially – it would seem – with Muslims! As with music, the content of any film watched should be acceptable Islamically[9]; this would probably rule out most, if not all, films with an '18' certificate (sex and horror films). Again, watching films shouldn't distract from prayer and other duties. If you're watching videos all day, the house is a mess and there's no dinner on the table for the family, there is obviously something wrong!

Most scholars seem to disapprove of cinemas and theatres. The content of a film or play may be acceptable, but the darkened atmosphere of the cinema or theatre may carry certain undertones which would make it unacceptable to Muslims[10] (one only has to think of the infamous "back row"). Especially in the West, most cinemas and theatres have bars attached, and many modern cinemas are to be found in leisure "complexes" which will include a variety of bars, clubs and discos – not really a suitable environment for Muslims. It may be noted that cinema attendance is regarded as improper, especially for women, in many parts of the Muslim world. If you're really keen to see a particular movie, remember that it will be out on video within months, and on TV in a year or two; you can watch it at home with the family in a much more wholesome atmosphere!

Laughter and Jokes

Muslims are not supposed to be miserable! One sometimes hears stories told of a time in Britain when older Muslims would scold younger brothers and (especially) sisters for even smiling. This is contrary to the Sunnah; the Prophet (SAAS) smiled a lot, and laughed too, although never in an undignified manner. Jokes are fine in moderation, as long as they do not involve lies, obscenity or mockery of other's misfortunes or shortcomings:

> "O you who believe! Let not some men among you laugh at others: it may be that the (latter) are better than the (former):
> nor let some women laugh at others: it may be that the (latter) are better than the (former): nor defame nor be sarcastic to each other, nor call each other by (offensive) nicknames..." (al-Ḥujurāt 49:11)

In his Tafsir of this Ayah, Bilal Philips points out that Islam strongly condemns verbal abuse, of all kinds, and that this Ayah, as well as warning the Muslims in general, reiterates the warning specifically to women – because women are just as prone to such shortcomings (some might say that we are more so!) as men[11].

Hobbies

There are many hobbies and pastimes which offer leisure and relaxation. As with other forms of leisure, they should not go against Islamic principles or take up so much time that they detract from other duties. Cooking, sewing and knitting are traditional women's hobbies which can be fun as well as being beneficial to the whole family, for obvious reasons.

Reading is another popular hobby – again the "content" criterion applies (put down that Mills and Boon!), but much can be learnt from books, whether they are specifically Islamic or not. Writing can also be a good way to spend leisure time; depending on what you can write about and which publications you can send it to, it can be a form of *Da'wah* or a way to earn a little extra cash. Letter-writing is also great fun, and it can be a way of strengthening the ties of Islamic sisterhood (if you write to Muslims) or an opportunity for Da'wah (if you write to non-Muslims) – obviously, a Muslim woman should not strike up a pen-pal correspondence with an unrelated man, just as she should not form a close friendship with male strangers.

Visiting

Muslims are encouraged to visit one another, to strengthen the ties of faith between them. It's especially important to spend time with fellow-Muslims when we live in a non-Muslim environment – this "fellowship" helps to strengthen our Iman. Many sisters, especially those who are married and at home (with or without children), may feel isolated during the day when husbands are out at work. Visiting one another is to be encouraged, as long as certain ground rules are kept to.

First of all, such socializing shouldn't keep you from your duties – make sure your own house is in order (literally!) before you leave it. If your house is in a state of chaos and there's no food prepared for the husband and kids in the evening, and you say it's because you "don't have time", you may well be overdoing the social activity, and it's time to reassess your priorities.

Secondly, visits to sisters should not be used to inspect their home furnishings for purposes of comparative snobbery; there will always be people richer and poorer than you are, so accept a sister for what she is, and don't judge her on the basis of her threadbare carpets! If you do come across a sister with a messy house, don't dismiss her out of hand, and don't gossip about her to others; instead, ask yourself the reasons why – is she ill? exhausted? depressed? Maybe she has just had her third/fourth/fifth child, or maybe she has been in hospital... – then roll your sleeves up, grab the Hoover and put sisterhood in action by giving her a hand!

Thirdly, gossip is not an Islamic pursuit, so if the talk at any gathering always turns to critical discussion of a person who isn't present, it's time to either speak out against such talk, or else leave and look elsewhere for more suitable company.

A good idea is to utilize social activities for Islamic purposes, so that they are less likely to turn into gossip-shops: a regular get-together could involve some study-time and/or Qur'an reading, so that everyone can gain some knowledge as well as enjoying "fellowship" with sisters in Islam. Alternatively, if the circle of friends include young mothers with small children, it can be an opportunity to bring Muslim children together and encourage friendship among them, and also teach them some Islamic songs or nursery rhymes. Such ideas extend naturally to organizing Eid parties or outings so that the children can really "feel Eid".

Da'wah

Da'wah, or inviting people to Islam, is a duty of every Muslim. We can utilize our "free time" for Da'wah purposes, as suggested above, but ideally our whole lives should be an example which will attract others to Islam – at school/college/work as well as among family and friends.

Da'wah operates on two fronts: towards Muslims who are perhaps unaware of Islam, maybe because of growing up in the west and missing out on a proper Islamic education; and towards our non-Muslim neighbours and colleagues, many of whom may be searching for Truth. At the very least, we may be able to counter-act the many incorrect stereotypes of Islam and Muslims; no-one else will do this for us – we have to speak up! and show by our behaviour what Islam is all about. By doing this, we may even bring people into the fold of Islam, in sha Allah.

Summary

Muslims aren't supposed to idle away their time in worthless pursuits, but almost all hobbies, sports and leisure activities can be turned into ways of learning, benefitting oneself or helping others, whilst relaxing and having fun at the same time.

Notes

1. Rehman, op. cit., p 374.
   Qaradawi, op. cit., p 292.

2. Hadith from al-Tabarani quoted by Qaradawi, p 296:
"Any action without the remembrance of Allah is either a diversion or heedlessness excepting for four acts: walking from target to target (during archery practice), training a horse, playing with one's family, and learning to swim".
3. Qaradawi, op. cit., p 293. Hadith from Ahmad and Abu Da'ud.
4. Qaradawi, op. cit., p 295f. Hadith from al-Bukhari and Muslim.
5. Muslim women are allowed to mix with non-Muslim women of good character, but some scholars suggest that they should not remove their Ḥijāb in front of non-Muslim women. See Mawdudi, *Purdah*, p 191.
6. See al-Kanadi, *The Islamic Ruling on Music and Singing*, p 31ff.
7. Qaradawi, op. cit., pp 300–304.
8. Qaradawi, op. cit., p 300.
9. Qaradawi, op. cit., p 306.
10. Qaradawi, op. cit., p 307.
11. Philips, *Tafseer Soorah al-Hujuraat*, p 90.

CHAPTER FIVE

Careers: Education and Work

There is much debate, among Muslims and others, about "A Woman's Place". In the West, the so-called liberation movement has succeeded only in placing a double burden on women's shoulders. Far from having a right to choose, women now feel obliged to run a household/have a family *and* pursue a full-time career. At the same time, whatever they choose to do, they feel compelled to explain themselves and risk accusations of being "lazy" or taking the "easy" option if they stay at home to have babies (ha!); or of being an "uncaring" wife and mother and/or "money-mad" if they go out to work.

Islam makes it clear that the woman's primary (but not sole) sphere of operation is indeed the home: she is certainly meant to be "home-based". However, those of us living in the west and/or influenced by western attitudes need to remind ourselves that Islam venerates the role of wife and mother. Far from being the lowly, second-best resort of the inadequate – as seems to be the common view in the west – it is regarded as the most honoured role for a woman. Interestingly enough, many non-Muslim western women (and not just "feminists") are beginning to fight back against this derogatory attitude and point out that being a housewife/mother is actually a very important job and also so difficult, demanding such a variety of skills, that no man could do it![1]

The question of staying at home vs. going out and about is not a new one: it occupied the minds of the first Muslim women too. A group of them once sent Asmā' bint Zayd to the Prophet (SAAS) to find out his answer to the problem. She told him: "I am a representative of a group of Muslim women who are supporting me. All of them hold the same opinion as I hold: that Allah has sent you to teach both men and women. We all believed in you and followed you. But the state of us women is this: we are tied to our homes; we are the centre of gratification of men's desires and bearers of their children. Men have been given preference in participation in Friday prayers, funerals and Jihād. When they go on Jihād, we look after their wealth and property, and nourish their children. O Allah's Messenger! Do we share in their reward and compensation (*thawāb*)?" The Prophet turned towards his companions and asked: "Have you ever heard a woman asking about her Dīn better than this woman?" They said: "By Allah! we have not". Therefore the Prophet (SAAS), addressing Asmā', said: "Go and inform those women that their good treatment of their husbands and seeking their satisfaction and supporting them for the sake of unity and solidarity (in the family), is the equivalent of all the men's services you have just mentioned"[2].

The role of mother is particularly valued in Islam, as is recorded in various Ḥadīth:

> Mu'awiyya ibn Jaḥmah (RA) narrated that Jaḥmah went to the Prophet (SAAS) and said: "O Messenger of Allah, I want to fight [in Jihād] and I have come to ask your advice." He said: "Do you have a mother?" Jahmah said: "Yes." He said: "Then stay with her, because Paradise is under her foot"
> (al-Nisā'ī, Ibn Mājah, al-Ḥākim and al-Ṭabarānī)

> Abu Hurayrah (RA) narrated: A man came to the Messenger of Allah and said: "O Messenger of Allah! Who is more entitled to be treated with the best companionship by me?" The Prophet (SAAS) said: "Your mother". The man said, "Then who?" The Prophet (SAAS) said, "Your mother". The man further said, "Then who?" The Prophet (SAAS) said, "Your mother". The man said again, "Then who?" The Prophet (SAAS) said, "Then your father"
> (Bukhari, Muslim)

However, there are women who are unable to bear children. This is a heartbreaking fact, especially for Muslim women whose culture is so child-loving, and who are expected by family and strangers alike to produce children. It is, of course, much easier said than done, but this fact needs to be borne with patience and faith. It is no-one's "fault"; Allah in His Wisdom chooses who will have children and when:

> "To Allah belongs the dominion of the heavens and the earth. He creates what He wills (and plans). He bestows (children) male or female according to His Will (and Plan), or He bestows both males and females, and He leaves barren whom He will: for He is full of knowledge and power" (al-Shūrā 42: 49–50).

Popular Muslim opinion sees all women as potential mothers, and it seems that people in general find it hard to understand that there are women who may never be mothers. Women who discover that they are infertile must not feel – or be made to feel – that they are some kind of "second class Muslimah". Motherhood is not the only role for a Muslim woman. Ayeshah (RA) herself never bore children, but is known as one of the "Mothers of the Believers" (an honorific title given to the wives of the Prophet SAAS); she was also a major channel of Islamic knowledge and a narrator of scores of Aḥādīth: eminent *Ṣaḥābah* and Muslims came from far and wide to consult her. Although she bore the sadness of never having children, she still had her part to play in the Ummah, she made a major contribution to Islamic knowledge, and to this day is venerated as one of the greatest Muslim women[3].

Knowledge and Education

Whatever role a woman is to play, whether a wife and mother or a career woman whose work is outside the home (or, indeed, both!), she needs knowledge. Seeking knowledge is a duty on all Muslims, male and female, so there is no excuse for denying Muslim girls and women an education. It's worth pointing out here that it is never too late to learn; even if you "missed the boat" first time around, for whatever reason, you can still make up for lost time. Classes and correspondence courses are available to adults in almost all subjects; libraries and their wealth of books and other materials are open to all – so there's really no excuse not to learn! There are even women's groups, up and down the country, running courses in confidence-building and employment-related training just for women. These groups exist because even western non-Muslim women may find training and working with men difficult, for many reasons. Such courses are open to all women, and some groups offer courses specifically for minority groups ("Asian", "Ethnic Minority", etc).

Knowledge can be roughly divided into two categories – "religious" and "secular" – although this division is not absolute, and may even be described as artificial: Islam has to do with all of life, not just formal acts of worship such as prayer and fasting.

Religious knowledge: In order to practise Islam, every Muslim needs to know at least the basics of prayers, fasting etc. Women also need to know how feminine conditions such as menstruation and post-natal bleeding affect their performance of these duties. It should also be pointed out that women need to be able to read Qur'ān too; some Muslim cultures seem to regard this as a boys-only area and neglect to teach their daughters – this is wrong. As stated above, it's never too late to start teaching your daughters, or to start learning yourself!

Secular knowledge: any job requires a certain amount of knowledge; the homemaker's task is certainly not one to be underestimated! A wife and mother needs to be as organized as any "professional", and to have many practical skills: cookery, sewing, basic first aid, secretarial skills, teaching, even (in this day and age) driving and house maintenance!

It's no exaggeration either to say that a mother needs a basic knowledge of virtually every subject you could think of, to deal with all those questions children will ask (failing that, you have to know where to find the answers: teaching children how to look things up in books is very worthwhile!). Children will ask about Allah (theology), why do stars shine (astronomy), where does Granny live (geography), why do things fall down (physics), and much, much, more... Western education will teach children to think and ask questions: it's no bad thing, but you have to be ready for it!

Of course it goes without saying that anyone who works outside the home will need to be suitably qualified for the job in question. In some cases, a Muslim woman will be at a double disadvantage, as a woman (so much for feminism in the workplace!) and as a member of a religious/racial minority; in this case a woman may need to be even better qualified than the white, male Brits who are after the same job. Being qualified for a job needn't necessarily mean having a long list of exam passes; experience and practical skills are just as valuable.

Work outside the home

Many Muslim women work outside the home for all manner of reasons: often financial, but also because a woman needs more stimulation than home life alone can offer her (especially in the west where the nuclear family lifestyle can lead to sheer loneliness and boredom), and/or she has a valuable contribution to make through her work.

This is in accordance with the example of the early Muslim women. Even the Prophet's wives were well-known for their skills in various fields; we have already mentioned Ayeshah's (RA) eminence as a scholar and transmitter of Ḥadīth; another wife of the Prophet (SAAS), Sawdah (RA), was expert in tanning and practised her craft[4].

Among the first Muslim generation were many women who worked. The trading activities of Kadijah (RA), the Prophet's first wife, are well known. Although she did not actually go out with the caravans of goods, she was a woman who was in control of her own wealth and business. Among the other women, some had their own fields and date-palm orchards, which they tended, and sold the produce; others ran businesses buying and selling in the market-place; still others were skilled in various arts and crafts[5]. Some of the women had medical and surgical skills and were able to tend the wounded on the battlefield[6].

From this we can see that Islam allows women to work outside the home, and regards them as capable at every intellectual and practical level. However, as Muslim women in a non-Muslim society we should be careful that whatever job or career we choose will not lead us to transgress Islamic limits; we should do our best to stick to Islamic dress and behaviour codes – the office flirting regarded as "harmless" by many in the west is not acceptable for Muslims. Our job should not involve handling alcohol (even to sell it or pass it to another person is considered Haram, in no uncertain terms), or excessive mixing of the sexes – dealing with men cannot be avoided totally in this society, but they should be kept to a minimum, and conducted in a brief and businesslike manner. Some jobs are obviously Haram: working in a bar or betting shop, for example. It's possible that a Muslim may find him/herself in such a job – a recent revert for example – in which case the best thing to do is hand in your notice and start looking for another job as soon as possible.

The so-called "caring careers" are often quoted as being best for women; there is certainly room for more Muslim women in these areas, especially in parts of the country where there are a lot of Muslims. These careers include:

Medical (doctors, nurses and auxiliary staff): doctors get all the glory, but the work of nurses and auxiliaries is just as valuable. Nursing is a "dubious" occupation in this country, where female nurses often have to treat male patients, but in some parts of the country it is possible to train as a midwife without going through general nursing training first. This is good news for those who are daunted by the prospect of nursing in mixed wards –

midwifery seems to be an area which interests Muslim women, and of course Muslim mothers would appreciate having Muslim midwives who would naturally know their concerns and cultural requirements. If you have already trained as a nurse (e.g. before reverting to Islam), you could choose appropriate specialities. Similar advice applies to anyone wishing to work as a nursing auxiliary: choose your ward with care!

Caring: social workers, counsellors. Muslim families have problems too, and there have been cases of gross insensitivity on the part of the social services: for example, two Jewish social workers were assigned to a Muslim family (in the event, they did their job excellently and didn't let any differences get in the way, but the family concerned did wonder if the social services couldn't have been more "diplomatic" in the choice of worker assigned!); in another case, a male social worker was assigned to deal with a Muslim woman and her children. Such cases of misunderstanding could be lessened if there were more Muslims in the social services; Muslim social workers themselves would be better able to help Muslim families, as they would understand cultural needs better; they would also provide a "bridge" between the people who need help and the services which are there for all, which Muslims pay for in their taxes, but which they may be unaware of. Counselling is an area which has really taken off in recent years (it can be done on a voluntary basis too, and training is available). While counselling can be very valuable, some counsellors may not take faith seriously – there is a need for counsellors who will take into account the importance of a person's faith when helping them work through their problems. When it comes to counselling people from religious/ethnic minorities, counsellors need to understand the everyday stresses of belonging to a minority – again, there is room for Muslim counsellors, of any racial origin.

Childminding: the ideal home-based job! Those Muslim women who have to go out to work are always on the look-out for Muslim childminders. For women who enjoy caring for children, this is an opportunity to help a sister, contribute towards a Muslim child's education (Tarbiya) and earn a little money for herself too.

Teaching: all levels, all subjects. Muslim schools are struggling with non-Muslim teachers, often of the "wrong" sex (male teachers in girls' schools, in particular), because of the lack of qualified Muslim staff. There is also a need for Muslim teachers in "mainstream" schools – they could set an example to Muslim students, and also promote a positive image of Muslims to non-Muslim students and staff – to counteract the sterotypes of TV and textbooks. There is a crying need for Muslim playgroups/nurseries and appropriately-trained staff: nursery work is traditionally a female preserve, and many courses are available – you can even study by correspondence for the Montessori certificate.

Dressmaking and design. There is definitely a need for affordable Ḥijāb – in all sizes and styles. Women who can design and/or sew could provide a service to other sisters, as well as making money from home. It's rather an ambitious suggestion, but a group of sisters could form a co-operative to make clothes and sell them by post – this would certainly help the more isolated sisters who aren't within easy reach of the few shops that do cater for women who wish to dress Islamically.

Arts and crafts: many people feel that Islam is "too dry" at present – when you look at the magnificent works of art in the museums, or see the old souqs, bazaars and mosques in Muslim cities, you wonder why Muslims aren't producing anything like that anymore. It has even been known for Muslims with artistic talents to be actively discouraged (by over-strict parents and others) from pursuing them, to the extent that they lose the gift which Allah SWT gave them. Every culture produces works of art; Muslims used to do so in the past, and there is no reason why they shouldn't do so again. Not every artistic medium is against Islamic law: we need artists (male and female) to enrich our culture within the bounds of Shariah.

Secretarial: there are Muslim bosses who would prefer a Muslim secretary but can't find one! There are many Muslim-owned businesses who need people with secretarial skills: it can be a very worthwhile and valuable job. However, sisters doing this kind of work must observe Islamic behaviour codes, and avoid Islamically unacceptable situations such as being alone in the office with a male colleague. Secretarial and typing skills can also be offered from home, especially with the advent of computer links, fax machines and other wonders of technology; people will always need documents, reports and theses typed up – this kind of work is also suited to working from home. So if you take a "career break" to have children, you can still fit some work in if you want or need to.

Media & Publishing; again, this is a field which may be suited to working from home – a freelance writer or editor can take on just as much or as little work as she wishes to fit in with domestic and childcare duties. In other fields, there is a need for more authentic Muslim voices, especially women: television and radio are the areas that spring to mind, but the "mainstream" newspapers and magazines are important too. There are some scholarships for trainee journalists and the like – you have to keep an eye on the papers (notably *The Guardian*'s Media section on Mondays). Some of the scholarships are for "ethnic minorities", so you can get in on the "ethnic ticket" if you must!

In Islam, all work can be considered as *'Ibādah* (worship), if you do it with a pure motive and seek the pleasure of Allah through doing your work well. Whether you're a housewife mopping the kitchen floor, a mother changing nappies or a high-flying manager of a successful company, your work is valuable. Whatever we do can provide opportunities for *Da'wah* as well, whether just by being seen to be intelligent, efficient and clean-living people, or more directly by talking to people we meet and answering the questions they may well ask. We should always be prepared to make the most of any opportunity that presents itself. At least we might make people think again about the negative stereotypes; at best we could be pointing the way to a better way of life for them.

Summary

Everything a woman does, whether she is a career-girl or a wife and mother (or both), is of great value. It has the potential to be counted as 'Ibādah (worship) for which we will be rewarded in the Hereafter, as well as deriving any benefits from it here and now – as long as we approach our work with the right attitude. Our work also presents us with opportunities for Da'wah which we must always be prepared for.

Notes

1. "What is a Housewife? (The Great Housewife Controversy)", *Good Housekeeping*, April 1992, pp 126–7. Just one example of the ongoing debate and strong feelings on the part of women and men alike.
   Faruqi, *Women, Muslim Society and Islam*, p 57, calls for an upgrading of domestic roles.
2. Rahman, op. cit., pp 89–90.
3. Rahman, op. cit., p 56; Siddiqi, *The Blessed Women of Islam*, pp 34–38.
4. Rahman, op. cit., p 162.
5. Rahman, op. cit., p 160 ff.
6. Rahman, op. cit., p 184.

CHAPTER SIX

Marriage

Islam regards marriage not as a "sacrament" but as a contract for life, which may – as a last resort – be dissolved by divorce. Marriage is intended not as an arena for the battle of the sexes, nor as a means of imprisoning women and treating them harshly, but as an institution which will offer security and stability to both partners and any children they may have.

> "...They [wives] are your garments and you are their garments..."
> (al-Baqarah 2:187)

There are certain guidelines laid down in Islam to help things run smoothly: first of all the way to find a partner, then the rights and duties of both husband and wife.

Finding a partner

The Islamic way of finding a spouse is usually described as "arranged" marriage. This does not mean that Islam condones the practice of forcing young girls into unsuitable matches, as the popular image portrays. What it does mean is that "dating" is not allowed in Islam; there should be no intimacy – not even holding hands or kissing – before marriage. The couple are allowed to see each other and meet, if they wish, but they must be suitably chaperoned.

The most important thing for women – especially younger women – to remember is that Islam gives you the final say in the matter: you have the right to say no. Young women may be very shy, but if you are really unhappy with your parents' (or guardians') choice of partner for you, you have to speak out; if you keep quiet, it will be taken as your consent to the marriage.

Abu Hurayrah (RA) reported that the Messenger of Allah (SAAS) said: "A previously-married woman must not be given in marriage without being consulted, and a virgin must not be given in marriage before her permission has been obtained". When asked how her permission was indicated, he replied that it was by her saying nothing"
(Bukhari, Muslim)

The normal Islamic cultural pattern is for the parents/family to find a spouse for their children, but many Muslims in Britain do not have that family support. Single people who have come here to study or work, or as refugees, may not have any family in the country. Reverts will almost certainly not be able to rely on their non-Muslim families to help them find a partner, so will need the help of their brothers and sisters in Islam.

For a single, previously unmarried Muslim woman who is without family to help her, the procedure is to have a Wakīl (guardian) – this should be someone who is well respected in the community; it may be the person through whom she embraced Islam[1]. The guardian should certainly be genuinely concerned for her welfare. Divorced or widowed women are allowed, in Islam, to manage their own affairs when it comes to arranging a marriage, but one is tempted to err on the side of caution and suggest it is better to have the support and advice of a close friend, especially for those who are new in Islam.

There is also the question of compatibility or equality of the potential marriage partners (*al-Kafa'ah*). The Islamic ideal is a "classless society" in which all Muslims are equal, and where the only level on which prospective couples need compare themselves is in their commitment to Islam. However, the scholars were aware of human nature and the fact that many societies are stratified into various levels and "classes", hence they recommended social equality in marriage, not as an absolute requirement – it may be waived on the agreement of both parties – but as a "rule of worldly wisdom"[2].

The criteria to be taken into account include not only piety, but also lineage, honour, and profession/level of education. The scholars advise that women should marry someone of equivalent status or above, but that men should marry someone of equivalent status or below. This is because the status of the wife and children will rise or fall according to the husband's position; if a woman "marries down", she may come to resent the loss of status, which will affect the stability of the family.

For women marrying within the community which they and their parents know well (whether in the UK or "back home"), finding out the status of a prospective husband should be comparatively easy. It is a different story for Muslims choosing an inter-racial marriage, especially for converts who may have an idealistic picture of Islamic egalitarianism and who may well be unaware of the traditional stratifications which exist in many Muslim countries. It is quite conceivable that women may find that they have married into a family so far "above" or "below" their own level that they suffer from a kind of culture-shock! There have also been cases of converts marrying men whose families are quite irreligious; these women then face the added burden of contending with the in-laws (let alone their own families!) disapproving of their Islam and pressurizing them in various ways because of it.

Whilst social equality is not an absolute prerequisite for marriage, any woman contemplating marriage would be well advised to think long and hard about the matter, and not be embarrassed or ashamed to include it in her list of criteria.

Living in the West, we must accept the fact that some marriages will occur along western lines, i.e. what are known as "love" marriages. We cannot adopt a judgemental attitude towards them; many people in the west – including Muslims! – know no other way, and if we as a community have failed to educate them, then we have no right to point the finger. Many revert women have come to Islam via a boyfriend/husband (some revert men may also have come to Islam via their spouses): we have to welcome them and help them bring their lives into line with Islam. Many, once they understand, are more than willing to do so. If the Muslim partner is sincere and willing to return to Islamic ways, then the couple have the opportunity to learn and grow together; if he is not, the woman may be better off without him! But whatever the case, she needs support, friendship and sisterhood from other Muslim women.

In the search for a spouse, there are also traps for the unwary. The following are being mentioned only to warn people to be aware, and the hope that the heartbreak may be avoided, insha Allah.

(1) Visa-hunters. British Muslim women may be prey to men who are less interested in a sincere Islamic marriage than in acquiring British nationality. Born-Muslim girls and their families have been known to be tricked

by men from "back home" who just want a stepping-stone into Britain. Revert women have also been fooled. Apart from the heartbreak caused, this abuse of Muslim cultural patterns gives a wonderful excuse to those who wish to see further restrictions on immigration, in which case it would be the sincere Muslims who would suffer. In the most extreme cases, the visa-hunting "husband" may treat his wife badly and cast her aside as soon as he gets his hands on a certificate of naturalization.

(2) Secretive polygamists. Islam allows polygamy, but British law doesn't! A second wife married only according to Islamic law would have no rights as far as the law of the land is concerned. In the interests of openness and fairness, both partners should show willing to marry according to both civil and religious law and/or be willing to discuss all arrangements openly and frankly; whatever is then agreed upon, as long as it is within the limits of Islam, is their own business. A prospective bride is entitled to know about any other wife, including any spouses "back home" (remember the "visa-hunters"!); a first wife should also know about any second wife. The author has heard of a case where – apparently unknown to all concerned – a man was married to two closely-related women at the same time, a state of affairs which is Haram. [It is not allowed for a man to marry two sisters, or a mother and daughter]. Whether the story is true or not, it is an example which illustrates the necessity for openness in marriage, especially in the case of polygamy.

Rights and duties

Islam gives us rights, as women and wives, but in asking for our rights we have to remember our duties as well. We can't expect to have all the privileges without being willing to shoulder our responsibilities too. (Of course, the men should be prepared to fulfil all their obligations as well, and not just enjoy the luxury of their privileges... but that's another book!) On the Day of Judgement, Allah SWT will ask us about what *we* did, not about what our fathers/brothers/husbands did. The rights and duties of a wife have been dealt with in great detail in many books and articles, and will be outlined again here:

Rights

The woman is entitled to food, shelter and clothing: this is what her husband must provide for her. What he provides must be equal to what he provides for himself; he cannot dress in designer clothes and expect his wife to wear jumble-sale rags! The wife is also entitled to fair treatment by her husband; she is not a target for abuse (mental or physical), but a companion to be cherished. These obligations are all summed up in the following Hadith:

> Bahz ibn Hakim reported: "I enquired of the Prophet (SAAS) about the instructions with respect to women, and he said: 'Feed them as you feed yourselves, clothe them as you clothe yourselves, and do not beat them or rebuke them"
> (Kanz al-'Ummal)[3]

Obligations

The wife's main duties, according to the scholars, is to preserve the integrity of the marriage; this can be regarded as falling into the following categories:

(1) **The sexual relationship**: the wife is not allowed to refuse sex to her husband. This is because, in Islam, marriage is the only legitimate outlet for the natural sexual urge. If you deny your husband this right, you may be forcing him to go beyond the bounds of Islam; we have to face the fact that in this non-Islamic environment there is a great deal of temptation around, and married couples need to help each other stay on the right path. Of course this right to sexual gratification is reciprocal: the wife has the same right[4].

(2) **Discretion**: the wife isn't supposed to discuss the family's affairs with anybody and everybody. In particular the couple's sexual relationship is intensely private and should not be discussed with anybody: this is in keeping with the Islamic concept of modesty. There are always people who will enjoy gossiping about our misfortunes or become intensely jealous about our successes; it's far better to keep the family's business in the family.

(3) **Obedience to the husband**: this applies not only in the matter of sex (see above), but in other areas too. The only instance where a wife can disobey her husband is when he goes against Islam: in this case obedience to the laws of Allah must take precedence over obedience to a man's demands – for example if a woman wants to fast Ramaḍān or pray, and her husband for some reason tries to discourage her. It's worth noting here that if you want to observe one of the non-obligatory

fasts, you need your husband's permission; this is related to the husband's right to satisfy his desire when he wishes.

Another area of obedience concerns one's social life: the husband has a say in who may or may not be entertained in the marital home, or indeed who the wife may mix with. Obviously, she should not mix freely with non-Maḥrem men, let alone invite them into the home, but there may be instances where the husband may disapprove of certain women. Only an unreasonable husband would deny his wife any social life at all, but if a particular individual is likely to cause some harm to the family, such as spreading gossip, exerting a bad influence or trying to disrupt the marriage in some way, the husband has the right to impose restrictions.

(4) **Fidelity**: It goes without saying that fidelity is required on the part of both husband and wife. The wife, in particular, is mentioned in the following Āyah:

> "Men are the protectors and maintainers of women, because Allah has given the one more (strength) than the other, and because they support them from their means. Therefore the righteous women are devoutly obedient, and guard in (the husband's) absence what Allah would have them guard. As to those women on whose part you fear disloyalty and ill-conduct, admonish them (first), (next), refuse to share their beds, (and last) beat them lightly; but if they return to obedience, seek not against them means (of annoyance): for Allah is Most High, Great (above you all).
> (al-Nisā' 4:34)

"What Allah would have them guard" is explained in the commentary as meaning that a wife should protect her husband's reputation and property, and her own virtue (Yusuf Ali note 546). A virtuous woman is faithful to her husband, and her behaviour reflects on the family; in many parts of the Muslim world, the family's "honour" stands or falls with the womenfolk's conduct.

Unfaithfulness, real or feared, on the part of the wife is the only instance in which beating the wife is allowed in Islam; even then it is the last resort, and is to be a mild beating only. The husband is *not* allowed to beat his wife because the dinner is late, the kids have wrecked the living room or he's just in a foul mood. Islam gives the woman the right to decent and fair treatment from her husband: there is no virtue whatsoever in submitting to such abuse.[5]

It is usually the case that the wife takes responsibility for most, if not all, of the domestic duties, although some scholars do not count housework as one of the wife's obligations. In a "traditional" set up, where the husband is at work all day and the wife is at home, it's only fair for the woman to do most of the domestic work – although husbands should follow the example of the Prophet (SAAS) and help out (if only occasionally!), especially if there are small children whose care in itself is a full-time job. Each family will have to work this out for themselves; if the wife is working, the husband should help or pay for help in the house, but as each case varies, there are no hard and fast rules. The following narrative may offer food for thought for all concerned:

> 'Umar ibn al-Khaṭṭāb (RA) said that a man came to his house to complain about his wife. On reaching the door of his house, he hears 'Umar's wife shouting at him and reviling him. Seeing this, he was about to go back, thinking that 'Umar himself was in the same position and, therefore, could hardly suggest any solution for his problem. 'Umar (RA) saw the man turn back, so he called him and enquired about the purpose of his visit. He said that he had come with a complaint against his wife, but turned back on seeing the Caliph in the same position. 'Umar (RA) told him that he tolerated the excesses of his wife for she had certain rights against him. He said, "Is it not true that she prepares food for me, washes clothes for me and suckles my children, thus saving me the expense of employing a cook, a washerman and a nurse, though she is not legally obliged in any way to do any of these things? Besides, I enjoy peace of mind because of her and am kept away from indecent acts on account of her. I therefore tolerate all her excesses on account of these benefits. It is right that you should also adopt the same attitude"[6].

Of course, quoting this does not condone anybody's excesses! We should all be making the effort to control bad tempers and angry tongues; at the same time, nobody is perfect. But this narrative gives us a brief insight into a marriage where there was a spirit of give-and-take on both sides; obviously there were ups and downs in the marriage, even arguments, but the marriage was strong and stable.

Summary

Marriage is supposed to be a joint effort; it is also something which takes time. Both partners should be prepared to make the marriage succeed, and not regard divorce as a quick way out when the going gets a little tough. If a marriage is to succeed, it needs a lot of give-and-take, a little bit of humour, and a deep commitment both to Islamic principles and to marriage as an Islamic duty. Much of this is embodied in the advice contained in the Qur'ān, Ḥadīth and other Islamic works; the rest is just common sense.

Notes

1. Darsh, response to author's query.
2. See Abdalati, *The Family Structure in Islam*, p 94.
3. Rahman, *Role of Muslim Woman*, p .
4. Rahman, op. cit., p 129.
5. Darsh, unpublished response to query from reader of *Usra – the Muslim Family Magazine*.
6. Quoted in Rahman, op. cit., p 149.

CHAPTER SEVEN

Divorce

Islam describes divorce as the most disliked by Allah of the things He has permitted. It is very much a last resort, a procedure only to be followed after all attempts to reconcile the couple have failed.

Prevention is better than cure

The best way to prevent divorce is to make sure that the partners are right for one another in the first place – this is one of the reasons behind the Islamic pattern of "arranged" marriage, where parents, family and other Muslims can guide the young people in their choice of partner, rather than leaving it up to the whim of youth, emotion and physical attraction, all of which are likely to be unstable bases for a marriage.

Having said that, however, marrying somebody just because s/he is known to be "A Good Muslim" is not enough! We are all brothers and sisters in Islam, but we don't all necessarily like one another or agree on everything – that's where faith and tolerance come in. There is also the matter of *Kafā'ah* (compatibility, equality). It is a rare couple who can overcome great differences in status, class, education, etc, especially if it is the wife who is deemed to be "higher" than her husband. While there is no "caste system" in Islam, it is advisable to select a partner of a similar background and level to your own. We have to go in to marriage with our eyes open and make sure we know what's what from the beginning. Sharing a commitment to Islam is the soundest base a marriage can have, but you have to look at the day-to-day considerations too. One hears of marriages where both partners are equally committed, but seek to express that commitment in different – and incompatible – ways. Could you cope with a husband's frequent absences for Da'wah purposes, for example, or cater for a constant stream of guests who are travelling around to proclaim Islam? Some of us would thrive on the constant company; others among us would crave desperately for peace and quiet... Some people are happy to marry partners of other cultures, and relish the challenge of fusing two ways of life to create an enriched, Islamic environment for the family. Others really would feel uncomfortable in a mixed marriage, and are much more at ease with a partner of a similar background. No one way is right. When it comes to marriage, keep your eyes open and follow your instincts. If you feel doubtful or hesitant for any reason, it may be better to err on the side of caution than to rush in to what may well be an unsuitable match.

You also need to have realistic views of marriage. It will take time to get used to one another, to adapt to one another's lives. It probably won't be a bed of roses from Day One! Marriage is something you have to work at; both partners have to give and take. Divorce is not to be used as a kind of "Panic button" the first time you have a row. Most couples do argue, it's part of the ups and downs of married life. Making a marriage work takes time; it's a bit like a pair of shoes – they get more comfortable as time goes by!

When a marriage goes wrong

However, for many reasons, marriages can go wrong. We are only human, after all, and can make mistakes in marriage as in all else; couples can sometimes grow so far apart that it seriously affects their marriage. When a marriage starts to break down, couples should try everything they can to bring about a reconciliation, but if it really is over, they are not condemned by Islam to a lifetime trapped in a miserable marriage. Divorce is the last resort. Contrary to popular myth, it is not a male prerogative to be used according to whim. There are various kinds of divorce in Islam; you can even have the right to divorce your husband written in to your marriage contract. Many women shy away from this right, but in these sad times one has to be level-headed and say it is well worth the precaution. Some men do abuse the institution of marriage and women should protect themselves, while at the same time being positive and willing to work to make the marriage succeed.

Either partner can initiate divorce proceedings, or else both may reach a mutual decision to separate. The different kinds of divorce in Islam are outlined below[1]:

Ṭalāq

This is divorce instigated by the husband. It involves a series of three pronouncements of divorce, but they cannot be given all at once, neither can they be given at the time of the woman's period[2]. The length of time between each pronouncement of divorce must correspond with the wife's monthly cycle (the timing of which varies from woman to woman, of course). In the meantime, every attempt must be made to save the marriage, and the wife is entitled to full maintenance from the husband.

A wife may have the right to divorce by Ṭalāq if this has been agreed upon before marriage and stipulated in the marriage contract. Many women feel too shy or reluctant to include this in their marriage contract but it is a right which has been given in Islam.

Khul'

This is another type of divorce which is initiated by the wife. In this case she must pay some form of compensation to the husband, i.e. returning the Mahr (dowry)[3].

The woman is given this option to free herself from an unbearable marriage. There are precedents in the hadith literature of women obtaining divorce by Khul' because they could no longer bear to live with their husbands[4]. No-one should have to stay in a marriage which has become a miserable torment, and which may push a woman beyond the limits of Islam.

The woman has the right to demand Khul', and although Islam generally discourages divorce, the man should, if all else has failed, let her go,[5] Sadly, nowadays, one hears all too often of marriages where the husband treats the wife with appalling cruelty, yet will not divorce her or allow her a divorce. Such men need to be reminded of the words of Allah SWT:

> "When you divorce women, and they fulfil the term of their ('Iddah), either take them back on equitable terms, or set them free on equitable terms; but do not take them back to injure them, (or) to take undue advantage; if any one does that, he wrongs his own soul..." (al-Baqarah 2:231)

Mubāra'ah

This is divorce agreed upon by mutual consent.

Li'ān

This is divorce in a case where the husband accuses the wife of adultery. In Islamic law, four (!) eye-witnesses are required to prove such a case. If he cannot prove it, the husband must swear by Allah four times that he is telling the truth. The wife is called to admit her guilt or swear to her innocence. Both must also invoke divine curses for swearing false oaths. If no proof (for or against) can be brought, the marriage is considered beyond reconciliation and will be dissolved.

Custody of children

Small children remain in the custody of the mother, unless she is obviously unfit to raise them. The father must provide full maintenance for the children, and compensate the mother[6]. The mother usually has custody of the children, unless she remarries[7], and in the case of children old enough to express themselves, their wishes should be taken into account too.[8] The children's interests are paramount; they should stay with the parent who is best able to care for them and bring them up in Islam.

IMPORTANT NOTE

These are very serious matters which can only be dealt with in outline in this book. Each case will have its individual complications and consideration. Any sister finding herself in such a situation is strongly urged to consult with a trustworthy scholar and reliable Muslims, as well as any appropriate agency (Muslim Women's Helpline, etc), before entering into a matter as grave as divorce.

Summary

Divorce is permitted in Islam, but is regarded as the last resort. Prevention – in the form of care in choosing a spouse and a serious commitment to making the marriage work – is better than the "cure" of divorce. Contrary to the popular idea of "Ṭalāq! Ṭalāq! Ṭalāq!", divorce may take several forms, and a serious attempt at reconciliation is earnestly recommended. Small children usually stay with their mother, but the father is liable for maintenance; custody of the children is determined by their own best interests.

Notes

1. al-Faruqi, *Women, Muslim Society and Islam*, p 72ff.
2. This is due to the prohibition on sexual intercourse during menstruation; the husband's mind might entertain the thought of divorce at this time because of frustration. See Qaradawi, *The Lawful and the Prohibited*, p 213.
3. See Qaradawi, op. cit., p 219.
4. Maudoodi, *The Laws of Marriage and Divorce in Islam*, p 36ff.
5. Maudoodi, op. cit., pp 40–41.
6. Abdalati, *The Family Structure in Islam*, p 246.
7. Rahman, *Role of Muslim Woman*, p 314.
8. Ibid.

CHAPTER EIGHT

Health

Everyone needs to have at least a basic knowledge of health and related matters. That doesn't mean we all need degrees in medical science, and those looking for in-depth diagnostic information will not find it in this chapter. What you will find is general information, observations and suggestions about health, medicine etc. as they relate to Muslim women.

Islam advocates a healthy mind in a healthy body, as we can see from various Aḥādīth about eating and drinking in moderation, taking some exercise/participating in sports, relaxing the mind with a little humour, etc (see pp 22–23). The physical benefits of the Ramaḍān fast are well known, as are the advantages of abstaining from pork and alcohol. What we need to learn more about are those areas which are not quite so well known and clear cut.

Medical examination and treatment

This is a matter which can give cause for concern, especially to sisters who wear Ḥijāb. The fact is that in this case, the normal rules regarding covering, touching, etc., can be waived. While it is possible – and preferable – to find a female GP, some specialist treatments may only be available from male medics. You may be able to get a referral to an all-female hospital in London for gynaecological treatment (The Elizabeth Garrett Anderson Hospital in Euston Road)[1], but if you need general abdominal surgery such as an appendix or gall-bladder operation, you're likely to be told that there are hardly any female surgeons in the country! When there is a need for examination and/or treatment by a doctor – including gynaecology and obstetrics – it is permissible for a Muslim woman to be seen by a male doctor. You can always take someone with you, or ask for a nurse to be present, as a "chaperone" – in fact many doctors themselves would prefer it this way. In such cases, only the part of the body which needs to be examined should be uncovered: a doctor who wishes to examine your stomach needn't see your legs; if you need medical assistance in childbirth, there is no need to uncover your hair or upper body. Most medical professionals are by now used to Muslim cultural needs (or are willing to listen to requests and usually welcome the opportunity to learn), and will respect them.

Medicines and treatments

The substances used in medicine must be things which are Ḥalāl (permitted). The only time when medication containing ordinarily Ḥarām substances may be used is in a case where there is absolutely no alternative and the non-use of the medicine would put the patient's life in danger[2]. This is obviously a rare situation: many of us suffer from complaints which, though inconvenient and maybe painful, are hardly life-threatening (chest and throat infections, iron deficiency/anaemia, etc). Many of the medicines prescribed in these cases come in capsule form: the capsules contain gelatine, which is of animal origin – the animal in question is rarely specified, however. Many medicines are available in alternative form – liquid or tablets – so it's well worth asking your doctor to prescribe an alternative; if none is available, however, there is nothing wrong in taking the medicine needed.

Herbal remedies

Herbal and other "alternative" or "complementary" forms of medicine seem quite popular among Muslims; this is no bad thing, as it may be that many of the chemicals used by the pharmaceutical industry are in fact harmful, and one can rest assured that herbal remedies are not derived from or tested on animals (the debate on orthodox vs alternative medicine is a complex one, and cannot be covered here; plenty of information is available to the interested reader). However, when seeking any form of complementary treatment, make sure the practitioner you consult is properly trained and is a member of a regulatory body – complementary medicine is not as rigidly controlled as the orthodox variety, and almost anyone can call him/herself an alternative practitioner without having appropriate qualifications: obviously, this can result in actual harm to patients[3].

Blood transfusions and organ transplants

These are allowed in Islam[4]; the scholars have long since debated and cleared up this question, but Muslims may well be confused about them, especially when they haven't given the matter much previous thought but suddenly find themselves in need of a blood transfusion as a result of an accident or severe blood loss during surgery or childbirth etc. Rest assured that it is allowed; you're doing no wrong by accepting a transfusion.

Organ transplants are also allowed in Islam, as the needs of the living take precedence over the dead. Many Muslims worry about the prohibition on harming the dead, but this actually refers to the barbaric practice of mutilating the dead on the battlefield[5], as was done by the pagan Arabs in battles against the first Muslims, not to a case where a bereaved family wish to help another person live by donating their loved one's organs. Agencies who deal with organ transplants are always appealing for donors; it's worth thinking the matter through now, and if you're willing to do so, make your wishes known by carrying the relevant donor card.

Nutrition and diet

Women need to have a basic knowledge of what foods are "good" and "bad", so that they can provide healthy meals for their families, and for themselves, of course! A good diet is also essential during pregnancy and while breastfeeding: it can make the difference between feeling fit and well or tired and run-down (although getting enough rest and moral and practical support from the people around you are also essential)[6].

We also need to be adept at label-reading, to make sure the foods we buy are Ḥalāl. A word of caution: the food companies often change their ingredients (according to fluctuations in the price of the various ingredients – they want to keep the price of the good they sell fairly stable, after all!). If you read a label one day and it looks fine, don't assume that that cake/pie/candy is Ḥalāl for evermore; an example is Opal Fruits – they used to contain gelatine, then for a while were "OK", but gelatine was subsequently reintroduced and at the time of writing they are not acceptable; it may change again in the future. Some brands, including many supermarkets' own labels now use specific symbols to indicate whether foods are "suitable for vegetarians" – the Vegetarian Society's own "V" symbol is the most reliable, as their conditions are the most stringent, but some supermarkets use their own symbol. Kosher meats and food are also acceptable, if you can find them: they are difficult to find in areas which don't have a large Jewish population. Foodstuffs imported from the US may have an unobtrusive "K" or "P" in a circle somewhere on the packaging. This signifies the fact that the food has been passed as Kosher by the Jewish religious authorities in America.[7]

It is hoped that Muslim women are too sensible to fall into the obsessive dieting trap, but this is a danger as many of us have grown up in the West and may be influenced by the pervasive media images of slim and beautiful people. This is a modern whim of western fashion – in past centuries in the West, the fuller figure was considered desirable[8]; indeed in other parts of the world, including some Muslim cultures, fat is seen as preferable to thin – in some Arabic dialects the words for "fat" and "thin" carry the connotations of "in good health" and "weak", respectively. The facts are that any such social pressure to conform to a particular body shape are quite unfair and unrealistic; we have all been created in different shapes and sizes, and most of us quite simply aren't meant to be a skinny size 8 or 10! Faddy diets are now widely acknowledged not to work, and most people who lose weight this way usually put it all back on, and maybe more, when they stop dieting, because their metabolism has been disrupted. Saying this does not mean that Muslim women have a licence to stuff themselves with food and get fat and lazy, far from it! Whatever our size and shape, we should still care for our bodies, eat properly and exercise regularly: women who are a size 16 plus can still exercise regularly, play sport and be fit and active. We should accept ourselves the size and shape we are, and not waste time and effort on trying to change to be what we are not; Muslim women have got more important things to do than fuss about their dress size!

IMPORTANT: If you are severely overweight and/or have a medical reason to lose weight, then you should take steps to reduce your weight: this is a matter of health, not idle vanity. Such weight-loss is better achieved by sensible eating (re-educating yourself about food, if necessary) and exercising regularly, but if you're not used to exercise, take it slowly at first – a gradual weight loss is better than losing it all quickly on the latest "wonder diet" and then putting it all back on again just as quickly.

Smoking

In a word, DON'T!! Smoking is bad news in both spiritual and physical terms. In the past, scholars wondered if it was *Makrūh* (disapproved) or *Ḥarām* (forbidden). Nowadays, with all the scientific proof that smoking is harmful and has no benefits whatsoever, there is no question that it is Ḥarām.

"And make not your own hands contribute to your own destruction" (al-Baqarah 2:195)

"Do not kill or destroy yourselves: for verily Allah has been to you most Merciful" (al-Nisā' 4:29)

"But squander not your wealth senselessly. Squanderers are, indeed, of the ilk of the satans"
(al-Isrā' 17:26–7)

Smokers may argue that it's their business, and they are harming only themselves, so what has it to do with anyone else? Unless you only ever smoke in designated smoking areas (such as on trains, in restaurants, etc), in the open air, or among other smokers, that is simply not true. The dangers of passive smoking – exposure to other people's smoke – is well documented; it's not only unpleasant for a non-smoker to have to breathe in other people's smoke, it's also a threat to his/her health. It is also the height of bad manners to smoke in the home of a non-smoker; the effects of the smoke will linger for several hours after your departure.

For women smokers, there's not just the danger of cancer, heart disease, and the like to yourself (the risks are increased by smoking, but if you give up, they soon decrease), there is also the threat you cause to your children, even before they're born.

Smoking in pregnancy can mean that the placenta doesn't work as effectively as it should, and this can deprive the baby of nutrition and oxygen. There is an increased risk of miscarriage, congenital abnormality, low birth-weight, etc[9]. If you smoke while pregnant, you are exposing your baby to needless risk. Children of smokers are also widely known to suffer more infections (ear, throat, chest) and may be at more risk of developing asthma. You have the choice whether to smoke or not, but if you smoke while pregnant or in the presence of your children, you're not giving them a choice at all!

It's better not to start smoking in the first place, of course. If you can resist any pressures or temptations, that's the best way to deal with it. Smoking does not make you look more ''glamorous" or "attractive", and it certainly won't help you if you feel nervous or depressed. The way to cope with negative feelings is first of all through prayer and putting one's trust in Allah; and also by finding a trustworthy and supportive friend or relative who can help. It's better to try and work out the root of any bad feelings, and deal with it directly, than hide behind a "smoke screen"!

If you are a smoker, the best Islamic advice is to give it up as soon as you can. Some people can give up in a day; if you find it more difficult, there is a wealth of advice available, from doctors, clinics and anti-smoking organizations such as ASH (Action on Smoking and Health) who want to help people kick the habit. You can even get hypnotherapy tapes and other forms of "alternative" help. Somewhere there must be a method that will help you! As with any other kind of "struggle" (remember *Jihād al-Nafs*, mentioned earlier in Chapter One), prayer and *Dhikr* (remembering Allah) will help, as will moral support from other people. The idea of better health, fresher breath, cleaner smelling clothes and more money to spend on good things will also give an added incentive: go for it!

Contraception

This is a thorny issue, and the source of much heated debate. The first thing to be said is that it isn't really solely a women's issue: it should be discussed openly between husband and wife, neither partner should seek to prevent conception without the knowledge of the other.

Islam encourages Muslim couples to have children, and offspring are regarded as a blessing, as well as a responsibility. No Muslim couple should seek to prevent having children indefinitely, although contraception is allowed in some circumstances[10]. Using contraception to "space" children is allowed, as is using it to prevent further children once a couple has had a family: the health of the mother must be taken into account – if she is unable to care for the children she has already, why should she undergo a further pregnancy? After a difficult birth, doctors may advise waiting a couple of years before having another child – this is in the interests of the mother's health, to allow her to recover fully; in some cases the mother's health, even her life, may be threatened by a further pregnancy, in which case it would be foolhardy to allow it.

Various methods of contraception are available, but not all are suitable for Muslims. The IUD or coil in particular should be avoided, as it is an abortifacient rather than a contraceptive: it allows conception to take place, but doesn't permit the embryo to embed itself in the wall of the uterus[11]. As abortion is strongly condemned in Islam (unless the mother's life is in danger), this is obviously an inappropriate method for a Muslim woman.

The Pill is also rather controversial: it can have side-effects, and may be damaging in the long term. It works by interfering with the body's natural cycle, i.e. by suppressing menstruation; the monthly "withdrawal bleed" experienced by women on the Pill is not a true menstrual flow.

It should go without saying that so-called "morning-after" pills should also be avoided by Muslim women. These are abortifacients which will kill the embryo, if conception has taken place.

Barrier methods (cap, sheath/condom) are possibly best, and closer to the particular way referred to in Hadith, i.e. 'Azl [coitus interruptus]. They do not disrupt the natural functions of the woman's body in the way that the coil and the Pill do.

There are also the so-called "natural" methods, which involve monitoring the "Basal Body Temperature" (temperature before getting out of bed or eating or drinking in the morning), which is recorded on a chart, and/or checking for changes in the nature of vaginal mucus. Changes can be indicative of ovulation, so a couple who do not wish to conceive can avoid marital relations around the time of ovulation; conversely, a couple trying for a baby can increase their efforts around this time. This method is particularly suitable for couples who wish to avoid any "artificial" form of contraception, but it is not foolproof (nor, of course, is any other method 100% reliable).

Pregnancy and childbirth

It cannot be over-emphasized that pregnant women should attend ante-natal classes and/or read widely about pregnancy, labour and afterwards. Giving birth is one of the most intense experiences you will ever go through, and it can be alarming if you do not understand what it happening. The more you know about how your body is working at this time, the better able you will be to cope with it.

It would seem that "natural" childbirth is a good thing, and that it is popular among Muslims; one aspect of the philosophy surrounding it which may particularly appeal to Muslim women is the objection to childbirth having been "taken over" by the male medical establishment, in the form of obstetricians! While this may sound like a rather radically feminist viewpoint, it is true that we prefer, and should have, only female attendants (apart from a brave husband!) during childbirth, as far as possible. The husband's presence at the birth is neither discouraged nor encouraged in Islam; it is a matter for the couple to decide according to local custom and their own wishes[12].

The natural birth movement encourages you to "go with the flow" and regard the pain of labour as positive and life-giving, not as a force to be resisted. This is all very noble, and some women can manage with the minimum of pain relief in labour, but there is a danger in all this heroism: those of us who do find the pain too much to bear, and/or find that we need medical intervention, may end up feeling as though we have in some way "failed". This is not the case; every woman, and every labour, is different. What will suit one will not suit another, indeed, in some cases the medical intervention is needed to save life (whether that of the mother or the baby); sometimes the baby may be in distress and any delay in bringing him out into the world could cause handicap or death. In such cases the woman who accepts "intervention" has most emphatically not failed, but has simply done what was necessary in her case. Try "natural" or "active" birth if you like the sound of it; if you find that when it comes to the crunch you need more help from the medical staff than you thought you would, accept it graciously and gratefully. Above all, remain positive and flexible.

Homebirths are particularly suited to Muslim families, because you are more likely to have only the female attendants you want. You can also have other female relatives around you, who might be "in the way" in hospital. But homebirths are really only advisable for those who are fit and able for them; if you've had any problems in pregnancy, or if a previous birth has been difficult, you should go to hospital. If your GP is opposed to home births, or prefers not to undertake such care, you can transfer to another GP for the duration of your pregnancy.

There are pros and cons to both sides in the home-vs-hospital debate; each woman must look at her own circumstances, health, housing, etc., and make her own mind up. Many hospitals are used to Muslims nowadays, so they're not as "daunting'' as they may have been in the past; most staff will be aware of Muslims' cultural needs, or will be willing to learn and respect our needs if we, for our part, take the trouble to explain things to them.

Breastfeeding

This is the recommended method for feeding your baby, as it has been specifically mentioned in the Qur'ān and Sunnah[13]. True, at the time of the Prophet (SAAS) there was no other method, and women who couldn't feed their babies themselves had to give them to a wet-nurse. But nowadays, health professionals have discovered – after a few decades of the "fashion" of bottle-feeding – that Breast really is Best[14].

Having said that, however, the new mother still has to be wary of the subtle pressures to bottlefeed which exist even though they have been told the right thing by midwives, health-visitors, etc. Free samples of babymilk are available in post-natal wards, and it is very tempting to resort to a ready-mixed, ready-sterilized bottle in the early days when nipples are sore and the baby hasn't quite got the hang of latching-on. Breast-feeding is a matter of demand and supply; the more the baby suckles, the more milk you will produce – it needs time, patience, a good diet, plenty of rest and lots of practical support from the people around you (husbands, please note!)

If for any reason you don't manage to breastfeed for long, don't despair; again, nobody should have to feel a "failure". Breastfeeding for a week is better than not at all; in the first few days the breasts produce a substance called colostrum which is of immense benefit to the baby, as it contains a high level of anti-infective substances[15]. Just by giving the baby breastmilk for those first few days you will have done him good. When you start bottle-feeding, make sure that all utensils are properly sterilized, and when preparing the milk, follow the instructions to the letter.

Subfertility and infertility

Subfertility means that a couple are able to produce children, but not as readily as others; such couples may never use any form of contraception, but may only produce two or three children, several years apart. Infertility means that one or both partners are unable to have children at all; it is a condition which takes time to come to terms with, and needs compassion and understanding on the part of others.

When a Muslim couple marry, they get a few weeks' peace before the "Is she pregnant yet?" enquiries start rolling in! In many Muslim societies, it is normal to start a family straightaway; this is not always the case in the West, for Muslims or non-Muslims. Many couples will come up with the good news everyone wants to hear within a year or two of marriage, but for some it takes longer. The questions then become embarrassing and even hurtful. The couple – especially the woman – will wonder what's wrong with them; they may resent the questions, which may be asked with sincere concern, but which can come across as being insensitive; and the anxiety felt may itself affect the woman's ability to conceive (there are cases of women who had thought themselves infertile, adopted a child and so started to relax about the whole issue of ever having a child... and then found themselves pregnant!)

A woman may, after a few months of failing to conceive, take herself off to her doctor to find out why. The thing to be aware of (the doctor will point it out too) is that infertility is not always the woman's "fault"! The man has a part to play as well, and if the doctor is to investigate the case and/or refer you to a specialist, he will need to check your husband out too. They will check your general health, ask about your work and lifestyle (work environments, such as dealing with hazardous chemicals, and lifestyle factors such as smoking, can all affect fertility), and check your reproductive organs. The tests and examinations can be embarrassing, but need to be gone through if you're to get to the root of the problem. You're not the first or only couple to undergo these tests, and most doctors will be sympathetic and discreet.

Many conditions can be treated, such as irregular ovulation in women, which can be controlled by drugs. Some conditions will require surgery, and you may even decide to choose in-vitro fertilization ("test-tube babies") and the like. Such treatments are allowed in Islam only if the sperm and eggs used come from the husband/wife. Using sperm or eggs from "donors" is Haram[16]. Most treatments will take time to work, so be patient and try not to get too anxious about it – the anxiety will not help, as the mind and body are so closely interconnected that the one may affect the other.

In many cases, treatment and time will do the trick; some couples who have been childless for years will go on the produce two or three children ("making up for lost time!" as one such mother called it). But others will find that there is no treatment for their condition; they are unlikely ever to become parents.

This fact is referred to in the Qur'an:

> "To Allah belongs the dominion of the heavens and the earth. He creates what He wills (and plans). He bestows (children) male or female according to His Will (and Plan), or He bestows both males and females, and He leaves barren whom He will: for He is full of knowledge and power"
> (al-Shūrā 42:49–50)

These couples may need time to come to terms with their situation and even – it has been suggested – to go through a process of grieving for the children they will never have. It is difficult for them to be surrounded by a child-loving and family (i.e. child) oriented society such as the Muslim community. People who seem to produce children easily may be unintentionally insensitive, such as a woman who may complain about being pregnant again(!) in the presence of another woman who may never have a child, but who longs desperately for that missed period and morning sickness. We need to be aware of, and sensitive to, other people's feelings, listen to them if they want to talk about it, and respect their silence if they would rather not. It is a difficult topic to write about, but that is no excuse for ignoring the problem: we all have to come to terms with it.

Summary

Health matters to Muslims. We should actively seek good health, through good diet and exercise; when ill, we should try to make sure that our treatment is within the limits of Islam as far as possible, but be aware that in some cases what is normally forbidden may be allowed. Women in particular need to be aware of the functions of the female body, menstruation, pregnancy, childbirth and breastfeeding; but having a good general knowledge of health matters will be of great benefit to themselves and their families.

Notes

1. At the time of writing, the future of this hospital as a women-only institution is in doubt. Muslims (and others) need to speak up so that the powers that be will realize that there is a demand and need for such facilities.
2. Dr. Taha, *Medicine in the Light of the Qur'an and Sunnah*, p 19.
3. Monthly magazines such as "Practical Health" etc, on sale in health food shops and some newsagents and supermarkets, would provide a good starting point for anyone wishing to know more about alternative therapy.
4. Darsh, *Islamic Health Rules*, p 3, Ta Ha, London.
5. Darsh, response to author's query.
6. Buckley, *Islamic Parenting*, p 4, 6. See also the various booklets and leaflets given out in clinics to pregnant women, which contain much sound advice.
7. "K" stands for "Kosher", "P" for "Parev", i.e. foods which are neither "meat" or "milk" (this relates to the strict Jewish dietary laws which forbid the eating of meat and milk at the same meal).
8. Bronsmiller, *Femininity*, p 29. In the twentieth century alone, the "fashionable" body [in the West] has changed several times between the voluptuous ideal of the turn-of-the-century to the androgynous "Twiggy" look of the 1960s.
9. Brook, *Naturebirth*, p 184, 185.
10. Darsh, "Question Time" (answers to readers' queries), *Usra – The Muslim Family Magazine*, Safar 1410 AH/September 1989; Qaradawi, *The Lawful and the Prohibited*, p 199f.
11. See for example: *Handbook of Contraceptive Practices*, Department of Health, p 43f; "Mother and Baby" magazine, September 1992, p 107. Thanks to Mrs. Victoria Gillick for supplying this information.
12. Darsh, response to author's query.
13. "The mothers shall give suck to their offspring for two whole years, if the father desires to complete the term. But he shall bear the cost of their food and clothing on equitable terms..." (al-Baqara 2:233).

    The following Hadith also offers encouragement and comfort to mothers of small children:

    > "Narrated Anas (RA): Sallamah, the nurse of his son Ibrahim, said to the Prophet (SAAS): O Messenger of Allah, you brought tidings of all the good things to men but not to women. He said: Did your women friends put you up to asking me this question? She said: Yes, they did. He said: Does it not please any one of you that if she is pregnant by her husband and he is satisfied with her that she receives the reward of one who fasts and prays for the sake of Allah? And when the labour pains come no one in Heaven or earth knows what is concealed in her womb to soothe her (to cool her eyes). And when she delivers, not a mouthful of milk flows from her and not an instance of

the child's suck, but she receives, for every mouthful and every suck, the reward of one good deed. And if she is kept awake by her child at night, she receives the reward of one who frees seventy slaves for the sake of Allah" (al-Tabarani).

See Schleifer, *Motherhood in Islam,* p 53.

14. Many books on breastfeeding are now available, and the parent-and-baby magazines abound with articles on the subject. Books include: *The Art of Breastfeeding* by La Leche League, *The Experience of Breastfeeding,* by Sheila Kitzinger, and *Breastfeeding: How to succeed,* by Derek Llewellyn-Jones.
15. Llewellyn-Jones, *Breastfeeding,* p 91.
16. Darsh, response to author's query. See also Qaradawi, *The Lawful and the Prohibited,* p 227f.
17. See Stanway, *Why Us?,* p 165ff.

Bibliography

ABDALATI, Hammudah: *Islam in Focus*, W.A.M.Y., Riyadh, n.d.

________, *The Family Structure in Islam*, American Trust Publications, 1977.

BADAWI, Jamal A.: *Al-Ṭahārah – Purity and State of Undefilement*, Islamic Teaching Center, Plainfield, Indiana, 1979.

________, *The Muslim Woman's Dress According to the Qur'an and Sunnah*, Ta-Ha, London, 1980.

BALASKAS, Janet: *Active Birth*, Unwin Paperbacks, London, 1983.

al-BAYHAQI, Imam, *The Seventy-Seven Branches of Faith*, The Quilliam Press, Dorton (Buckinghamshire), 1990.

BROOK, Danaë, *Naturebirth: Preparing for natural birth in an age of technology*, Penguin (sorry!), London, 1976.

BROWNMILLER, Susan, *Femininity*, Paladin, London, 1986.

BUCKLEY, Silma: *Islamic Parenting, The Natural Alternative*, Muslim Converts' Association of Singapore, 1991.

al-BUKHARI: see KHAN

DOI, Abdur-Rahman: *Women in Sharī'ah (Islamic Law)*, Ta-Ha Publishers, London, 1989 (2nd ed).

al-FARUQI, Lamya': *Women, Muslim Society and Islam*, American Trust Publications, Indianapolis, 1408/1988.

FAZLUL-KARIM, Al-Haj Maulana: *al-Hadis* (4 vols), The Book House, Lahore, n.d.

HUTCHINSON, Sarah: *The Hijab in Classical and Modern Muslim Scholarship*, unpublished PhD thesis, School of Oriental & African Studies, London University, 1987.

IMRAN, Muhamad: *Ideal Woman in Islam*, Islamic Publications Ltd, Lahore, 1981 (2nd ed).

al-KANADI, Abu Bilal Mustafa, *The Islamic Ruling on Music and Singing in the Light of the Quraan, the Sunnah and the Consensus of our Pious Ancestors*, Abul-Qasim Bookstore, Jeddah, 1991.

al-KANADI, Abu Bilal Mustafa, *The Islamic Ruling Regarding Women's Dress According to the Quran and Sunnah*, Abul-Qasim Publishing House, Jeddah, 1991/1411 AH.

AL-KAYSI, Marwan Ibrahim, *Morals and Manners in Islam: a guide to Islamic Adab*, The Islamic Foundation, Leicester, 1986.

KHAN, Ghulam Mustafa, *Personal Hygiene in Islam*, Ta-Ha/Islamic Medical Association, London 1982.

KHAN, Dr Muhammad Muhsin: *The Translation of the Meanings of Sahih al-Bukhari*, Kitab Bhavan, New Delhi, 1987 (Rev. ed.).

KITZINGER, Sheila, *The Experience of Breastfeeding*, Penguin, London, 1979.

LA LECHE LEAGUE INTERNATIONAL: *The Art of Breastfeeding*, Angus & Robertson, North Ryde NSW/London, 1988.

LEMU, B. Aisha and HEEREN, Fatima: *Women in Islam*, Islamic Council of Europe, UK, 1978.

LLEWELLYN-JONES, Derek, *Breastfeeding: How to succeed*, Faber & Faber, London, 1983.

MAUDOODI, Maulana Abul A'ala: *The Laws of Marriage and Divorce in Islam*, Islamic Book Publishers, Kuwait, 1993.

MAWDUDI, Syed Abdul A'ala: *Purdah and the Status of Woman in Islam*, Markazi Maktabi Islami, Delhi, 1981 (2nd ed).

PHILIPS, Abu Ameenah Bilil: *Tafsir Soorah al-Hujuraat*, Tawheed Publications, Riyadh, 1988/1409 AH.

al-QARADAWI, Yusuf: *The Lawful and the Prohibited in Islam (al-Halal wal Haram fil Islam)*, Shorouk International, London, 1985.

al-SABBAGH, Dr Abdullah Tawfiq: *Al-Hayd wa'l-Nifas, Dalil al-Mar'ah al-Muslimah fi'l-Dima' al-Fitriyyah*, Makatabat al-Nur, Heliopolis, Cairo, nd.

SARWAR, Ghulam: *Sex Education: The Muslim Perspective*, The Muslim Educational Trust, London, 1989.

SCHLEIFER, Aliah: *Motherhood in Islam*, The Islamic Academy, Cambridge, 1986.

SIDDIQI, Muhammad Saeed: *The Blessed Women of Islam*, Kazi Publications, Lahore, 1982.

STANWAY, Dr. Andrew: *Why Us? a common-sense guide for the childless*, Granada, St. Albans, 1980.

TAHA, Dr. Ahmed: *Medicine in the Light of the Qur'an and Sunnah*, Ta-Ha, London, 1993.

Glossary

AḤĀDĪTH: Plural of Hadith, qv.

'AWRAH: that which must be covered according to the Islamic dress code.

DĪN: way of life, religion.

DU'Ā': supplication, "private prayer, which may be in Arabic or one's own language.

DUPATTA: filmy headcover worn with shalwar-khameez (qv).

GHUSL: full ablution.

ḤADĪTH: narration of the sayings and deeds of the Prophet SAW.

ḤAJJ: Pilgrimage to Makkah, performed once a year during the Islamic month of Dhū'l-Ḥijja; this is one of the five pillars of Islam, and should be performed once in a lifetime by every Muslim who is able to do so.

ḤAYḌ: menstruation, monthly period (see chapter 00 on Tahara).

ḤIJĀB: the Islamic dress code and related attitudes; the word is also frequently used to refer to the head covering.

'IBĀDAH: worship.

IMĀM: leader, especially of congregational prayers.

IMĀN: faith, belief.

IQĀMAH: call to prayer immediately preceding the congregational Salat; the words differ slightly from those of the Adhan or call to prayer given to announce the ...

ISTIḤĀḌAH: non menstrual bleeding from the vagina.

KA'BAH: the cube-shaped building in Makkah which is the focal point towards which Muslims throughout the world face in prayer.

KHUṬBAH: sermon, speech, especially the sermon given during the Friday (Jum'ah) prayers.

MADHHAB: school of thought in Islamic jurisprudence; the four schools (named after their founders) are: Hanbali, Maliki, Hanafi and Shafi'i.

MAḤREM: a close relative to whom marriage is prohibited and before whom the rules of Hijab may be relaxed (i.e. father, brother, son, grandfather, uncle, nephew).

MUKALLAF: adult, responsible.

MUṢḤAF: a copy of the Qur'an in Arabic.

NIFĀS: post-partum bleeding, which may last up to forty days after giving birth.

ṢAḤĀBAH: The Companions of the Prophet Muhammad (SAW).

ṢALĀT: "formal" prayer, the five daily prayers which must be recited in Arabic.

SHALWAR-KHAMEEZ: traditional form of dress from the Indian subcontinent, a suit consisting of loose trousers and long shirt or dress.

SUNNAH: the practice of the Prophet SAW.

TAḤĀRAH: purity, state of undefilement, in a ritual sense.

TAKBḬR: pronouncing the phrase "Allahu akbar" (Allah is most great). The Takbīrāt-al-Eid are certain phrases in praise of Allah which are customarily recited by the congregation before the Eid prayers.

TASHAHHUD: that part of the Salat in which a person sits and recites "Al-Tahiyyatu Lillahi...".

ṬAWĀF: circumambulation (walking round) the Ka'ba, one of the major rites of Hajj and 'Umra.

'UMRAH: the "lesser Pilgrimage" which may be performed at any time of year.

WUḌŪ': partial ablution, to be performed after passing wind, urine, stools, etc.

Index